Mukteshwari

Mukteshwari

Aphorisms by
SWAMI
MUKTANANDA

A SIDDHA YOGA PUBLICATION
PUBLISHED BY THE SYDA FOUNDATION

Acknowledgments

Grateful appreciation goes to Cheryl Crawford for her cover and text design, to Steve Batliner for typesetting, and to Indu Kline, Sushila Traverse, Osnat Shurer and Martha Calderón for preparing the text for publication.

Photos of Bhagawan Nityananda and Swami Muktananda by Gadhekar.

Copyright © 1995 SYDA Foundation.® All rights reserved

(Swami) MUKTANANDA, (Swami) CHIDVILASANANDA, GURUMAYI, SIDDHA YOGA, and SIDDHA MEDITATION are registered trademarks of SYDA Foundation.®

Printed in the United States of America

First published in English as two volumes in 1972 and 1973
Second edition 1995

No part of this material may be reproduced or transmitted in any form or by any means, electronic or mechanical, including photocopy recording, or any information storage and retrieval system, without permission in writing from SYDA Foundation, Permissions Department, 371 Brickman Rd., PO Box 600, South Fallsburg, New York 12779-0600, USA.

Muktānanda, Swami, 1908-
    [Muktesvarī English]
    Mukteshwari : aphorism / Swami Muktananda. — 2nd ed.
       p.   cm.
    ISBN 0-911307-35-4 (alk. paper)
    1. Spiritual life—Hinduism.   I. Title.
BL1228.M82513   1995
294.5'4—dc20   95-15966
                                                             CIP

Contents

Note on the Genesis of Mukteshwari	ix
Preface to the Revised Edition	xiii
Preface to the First Edition	xxiii
Dedication	xxvii

I. All Is Nityananda — 1

II. Inner Self
You Yourself Are What You Seek	12
The Bliss of the Atman	24
The Self Reveals the Self	30

III. Kundalini
Awakening Chiti Shakti	34
Play of Chiti Shakti	40

IV. Yoga and Worldly Life
Value of Human Birth	46
Giving and Receiving	47
Status, Wealth, and Power	49
Speech	54
The Human Body	55
Food	60
Love	62
Loyalty	66
Dharma	69
Adharma	77
Divinity Revealed	82
The Pure Self in the World	85

V.	**The World Is as You See It**	
	Divine Eye	88
	Faulty Eye	93
VI.	**Destiny and Time**	101
VII.	**Knowledge**	
	Student, Teacher, Knowledge	108
	Receive God's Message	111
	Inner Knowledge, Outer Knowledge	116
VIII.	**Mind, Meditation, Japa**	
	Mind	126
	Path of Meditation	133
	Fruits of Meditation	139
	Meditation on Your Self	143
	By Japa, Life	148
	Natural Japa	152
IX.	**Guru**	
	Marks of a True Guru	162
	Marks of a False Guru	167
	Guru's Grace	170
	God, Guru, and Self	182
X.	**Disciple**	
	Worthiness	190
	Tests of Truth	195
	One-Pointedness	199
	Surrender	206
	Devotion	210
XI.	**Land of Yoga**	
	Ganeshpuri	214
	Ashram Dharma	217
	Yajna	225

XII.	Noble Life	
	Control of the Senses	228
	Brahmacharya	232
	Renunciation	237
	Reverence	241
	Self-Effort	244
	Self-Surrender	245
XIII.	Pitfalls	
	Bad Company	248
	Those Who Use Yoga for Unworthy Ends	250
	Siddhis	255
XIV.	The World Is God	
	Look upon Everyone as Divine	264
	The Many Are One	272
	Equality-Consciousness	276
	God's Caste	280
	Play of Reality	284
	Guru's Eye	291
XV.	Blue Light	297
XVI.	Jivanmukta	
	Siddha	308
	Jnani	311
XVII.	Know Your Self	
	Yourself and Your Divine Self	314
	Compassionate Sri Nityananda	324
	Guidemap to Holy Sites	331
	Guide to Sanskrit Pronunciation	332
	Glossary	333

NOTE ON
THE GENESIS OF MUKTESHWARI

During the celebration of his sixtieth birthday in May 1968, Swami Muktananda gave his devotees the gift of a small book on *āshrama dharma,* a guide to beneficial living in the ashram. The volume ended with a set of 61 verses, one for each of his years and one for the year to come. The devotees were overjoyed. And they asked for more. Baba responded with a promise of 1008 verses.

In the days that followed, Baba — as Swami Muktananda was called by his devotees — sat writing in Guru Chowk, the courtyard of his ashram in Ganeshpuri. This became a familiar sight to the ashramites as they went back and forth across the square — to the Nityananda Temple, to the meditation cave and gardens, to chanting, and to their *sevā,* or selfless service. In full view of everyone, inspired, unhesitating, Baba poured forth *Mukteshwari.*

Five-hundred-and-one of these verses were published on the auspicious day of *Shivarātrī,* February 15, 1969.

MUKTESHWARI

The remaining verses came out as a second volume on August 15, 1973, to celebrate the anniversary of Baba's initiation by his Guru, Bhagawan Nityananda.

During the early years of the 1970's, Westerners who had journeyed to Ganeshpuri to receive initiation from Baba, to study his teachings, and to participate in the rigorous spiritual practices of the *Gurukula,* often asked for translations of his books. Baba agreed, and in 1972 and 1973, *Mukteshwari* Volumes I and II were published in English.

For more than twenty years, these two volumes of invincible wisdom have inspired and nurtured the followers of the Siddha path. *Mukteshwari* is practical, straightforward, mystical, funny, sublimely lyrical, and filled with Baba's ecstasy. Over the years, there have been many requests to publish all the verses in one book, and the present volume is a response to that wish. For this new revised edition, the poet George Franklin has lovingly polished the translation, and Cynthia Kline, who was a student in Gurudev Siddha Peeth at the time *Mukteshwari* was originally published, has provided a map showing many of the places Baba refers to, a glossary, and a pronunciation guide.

For Baba, the names of God as well as the names of holy places, holy rivers, and holy beings, were the mantras of daily speech. Recitation of divine Names is a form of worship for a Siddha, and, whether we understand their literal meaning or not, the feeling they invoke in him is transmitted directly to us through their sound vibrations. To maintain the poetic flow of the aphorisms, we have not differentiated between Sanskrit, Hindi, and English words in setting the text. Unfamiliar

Note on the Genesis of Mukteshwari

names and all Sanskrit terms, however, are identified and explained in the glossary.

Mukteshwari, arising from a time of celebration, carries the joyful generosity of the original gift. We are grateful for the privilege of presenting it in this form.

Jane Ferrar
Shree Muktananda Ashram
New York, January 1995

Swami Muktananda

Preface
to the Revised Edition

It is monsoon time in India. The hills are covered with tall shoots of tender grass that wave in a moist breeze. The lush foliage of the forest trees is glistening with rain.

As we drive through the Kasara Valley on our way from Nasik to Ganeshpuri, I remember the stories of how as a young *sādhu* Swami Muktananda wandered over these hills with nothing but a loincloth and a thin shawl to protect him from the elements. As I look out onto the exquisite landscape, I imagine him sitting on the rocks by the river that flows through this valley, his mind and heart absorbed in joyful contemplation of God and His creation.

The only child of loving parents, Baba Muktananda left home and began to search for God while still a boy. Writing about this in *Mukteshwari*, Baba says:

> I wandered ceaselessly
> since childhood, always alone.
> I went to many places

and met many great beings.
Still I wandered on. [v.16]

Muktananda was not looking for a learned teacher of the scriptures or for one who could impart to him a few yogic techniques. He was in search of a *Sadguru,* a true Master, who could give him the ultimate, permanent experience of God, of the Self, of supreme love.

Baba describes his longing when he writes:

> I wandered throughout India
> searching continuously for my Gurudev.
> I ate mud when I had no food. [v. 18]

When he was without clothes or a blanket, and when he had no shelter, he covered himself with a *dargah* sheet, a shroud. "But," Baba writes, "I did not lose courage."

These hills remind me of Baba's indomitable resolve. As we drive along the valley, I ask, "What gave you such beauty, O hills and grass?" And they seem to answer, "Muktananda's seeking, his burning love for God, have given us our splendor." The whole valley is aquiver with maternal love for this extraordinary young man, the passionate seeker whom she nurtured and sheltered so many years ago.

Drunk with the beauty of God in which he reveled from those days on, Baba writes:

> Out of love
> the earth brings forth nectarean food.
> Out of love
> seasons change.
> Out of love
> the wind blows tirelessly. [v. 205]

Preface to the Revised Edition

That unconditional love is all Baba sought. Having attained it, sitting, talking, walking, eating, or sleeping, Baba remained the embodiment of love itself, and gave nothing but love to others. He writes:

> The Guru is love...
> Muktananda,
> drink deep of the Guru's love
> and become deathless. [v. 668]

Only when a seeker receives the Guru's grace is he able to drink so deeply of the Guru's love that he becomes immortal. Baba says over and over again that there is no spiritual attainment without the grace of the Guru.

> On the path of spirituality and peace
> the Guru is foremost.
> Without him there are only barren seeds. [v. 544]

Baba knew this from his own experience. When he was just a boy, the God-intoxicated saint Bhagawan Nityananda came to his school on a casual visit. It was a brief meeting, yet in those few moments Baba's heart was set ablaze with an intense longing to know God.

He began to search for a Guru. And as he searched, walking across the length and breadth of India three times for eighteen long years, Baba mastered many traditional yogic disciplines and skills — from *hatha yoga* to *ayurvedic* medicine and cooking. He became well-versed in the scriptures of Vedanta at the ashram of Siddharudha Swami at Hubli, where he was also initiated into *sannyāsa,* or monkhood. None of this satisfied his restless soul, and the ardor of his longing was undiminished. He continued to seek out the great spiritual beings of the time, until one day a saint told him that his "treasure" was lying in Ganeshpuri.

Arriving at Ganeshpuri, a tiny village in a remote jungle region of Maharashtra State, Baba was greeted by Bhagawan Nityananda, the great Siddha Master he had met briefly years ago at school, with the words, "So you have come." Baba had found his Guru. Bhagawan Nityananda bestowed upon Baba the sacred initiation of the Siddhas known as *shaktipāt,* by which the inner divine energy is awakened. It was a meeting whose outcome would fulfill the spiritual destiny of thousands of seekers in the glorious years that followed.

As a disciple, Baba followed the instructions of his Guru during a nine-year period of intense spiritual practices and inner purification. Then one day, dancing in ecstasy, Bhagawan Nityananda proclaimed, "Muktananda has become Parabrahman!" Bhagawan Nityananda had three rooms built for Baba on the outskirts of Ganeshpuri and asked him to stay there. This is what has grown into Gurudev Siddha Peeth, an ashram founded and run according to the inspiration of the ancient *Gurukulas,* where devotees pursue their *sādhana* in an atmosphere of discipline and tranquility.

On his three world tours, undertaken at the command of his Guru, Baba awakened the divine *Kundalinī* energy in countless seekers, giving them a taste of the supreme bliss in which he constantly reveled. Never before had a Master awakened the inner energy in so many seekers. Baba kept giving and giving. In this book he says, "Give freely, as God gives... Always give freely, withholding nothing. You will reach God."

The *Shiva Sūtra Vimarshini,* a profound text of Kashmir

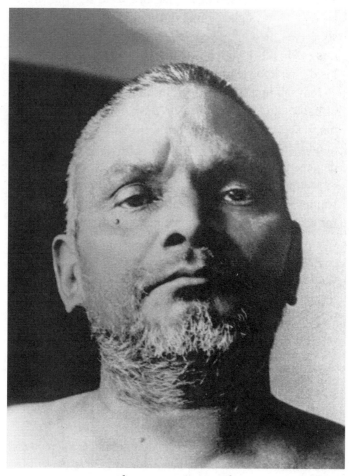

Bhagawan Nityananda

Shaivism, the philosophical tradition that Baba dearly loved, says, "As the moon, pure like a flower, shines all around, its rays gladdening the world in an instant, even so, O Parvati, a great yogi, moving from place to place on this earth, fills it with bliss through the moon-like rays of his divine knowledge."

I myself first had the good fortune of receiving the gift of Baba's divine *darshan* in 1973 when he was on one of his visits to Delhi. I was sitting beneath a colorful tent amid a huge crowd of devotees. Although I was not a devotee then, I couldn't help being affected by the air of expectancy that surrounded me. So many hearts were waiting to be filled! Imperceptibly, I, too, began to yearn for some blessing. All of a sudden, a feeling of cool stillness flowed into the area.

A few moments later, Swami Mutkananda strode into the tent, and as I watched him something broke loose inside me. A fountain of white, incandescent light burst upward within me. All the questions that had haunted me —Who was I? Was there any meaning to life? Did God exist? Could I experience Him?—came rushing up like foam atop this fountain of white light, then finally dissolved above it. In truth, though, there was no 'above.' There was only a limitless expanse of dancing, playing, shimmering white light. And that light was me!

Wherever I looked I saw only that radiance. Then, after a few moments, the light began to condense back into shapes and forms, into the solid-looking objects that I had observed before Baba Muktananda entered the tent. I felt that the secret of life, and of my own essential Self, had been revealed to me. The purpose and the goal of my existence became clear, and it was clear too from the

Preface to the Revised Edition

great experience that Baba had just given me that he had the power to take me to the permanent experience of the bliss of the Self. I reasoned that Baba could only have given me, in a mere instant, an experience so absolutely fulfilling and so final if he himself embodied it. For me he was God, he was the Guru, and I decided to follow him and his teachings.

Up until his very last days, Baba gave to others his supreme gift, the gift of the experience of God, the experience in which he himself always lived. Even then, Baba spent many hours a day in the Dhyan Mandir, the temple of meditation adjoining his own living quarters. There, by means of his divine touch, he would give *shaktipāt* to everyone who came to receive this most auspicious of all blessings.

Just a few months before his *mahāsamādhi*—the final merging of his consciousness with the cosmic consciousness of the eternal Self at the time of death—Baba entrusted the power of the lineage of Siddha Masters to Swami Chidvilasananda.

Having completed the path of discipleship himself, Baba writes:

> A perfect disciple...
> lives according to Sri Guru's commands,
> loves his Guru in thought, word, and deed,
> considers his Guru to be God,
> and knows no other God.   [v. 661]

Swami Chidvilasananda was such a disciple, and Baba gave her the state that he himself had attained. His gift to her was a gift to all of us. Gurumayi, as Swami Chidvilasananda is known to her devotees, travels all over the world as Baba did, transforming the lives of countless seekers. Through the gift of *shaktipāt*, both Gurumayi and Baba have enabled thousands of people to experience their own greatness.

Baba often said that he did not teach people because he thought they were small and helpless, but because he saw God in them and wanted them to recognize their own divinity. When Baba wrote the verse aphorisms of *Mukteshwari,* he was established in the state of God-realization. For a realized being, everything is his own Self. That is why, as Swami Prajnananda explains in her preface to the first edition of *Mukteshwari,* Baba addresses us in these poems using his own name, saying, for example, "Muktananda, the supreme Being is you." Many of the great poet-saints of India, whose verses Baba revered and contemplated his whole life, employed the same convention, addressing spiritual aspirants as if speaking to themselves, while giving them words of wisdom, support, encouragement, and inspiration.

How fortunate we are to be receiving such words from Baba! The very fact that this book is now in your hands indicates that you are stepping onto the path of grace and that your wandering is about to end. It is by Baba's grace that you are about to read his words. Understand that the words of a Guru are sacred mantras. When Baba gave the mantra to seekers he said, "Treat it like gold." With the knowledge that one word from the Guru can liberate us from bondage, let us treasure this book and the teachings contained in it.

For those seekers fortunate enough to read it, this book provides inexhaustible nourishment and guidance. Baba shares with us the passionate longing of his early years of

Swami Chidvilasananda

sādhana, as well as the poignant moments of divine revelation, the peaks of spiritual ecstasy that he experienced through the grace of his Guru. Talking to us as intimately as our own dearest friend, he says:

> In his journey through life
> a man meets many people who appeal to him
> and become his friends.
> Some friendships are short, others long.
> But only the Sadguru
> is a true and lasting friend,
> only he truly deserves this name.   [v. 545]

This book is a priceless gift from such a true and lasting friend. Let us fill our minds and hearts with the grace that come from its words.

Swami Madhavananda
Gurudev Siddha Peeth
Ganeshpuri, India
January 1995

Preface
to the First Edition

Mukteshwari is the poetic play of Muktananda, of Mukteshwar, as Shakti is of Shiva and Neela of Neeleshwar. It is the random harvest of the spiritual grains from the fertile field of our Gurudev's inexhaustible knowledge. These verses are rich with immortal truths to nourish, strengthen and satisfy the souls of seekers. They are universal truths, not limited to any one time, country, or sect. They belong to all true religion.

Mukteshwari is for Muktananda; it is addressed to him. And who is Muktananda? Muktananda is you. Gurudev addresses you as "Muktananda," thus making you one with him. He does not sit on a high pedestal to advise or lecture you, giving you the feeling of his superiority. He makes you feel that he is just like you. Indeed, in *Mukteshwari,* Muktananda is you and Nityananda is God within you.

Mukteshwari is Gurudev's message to mankind. Whatever subject he illuminates, rings with the reminder to turn within, to seek the imperishable divine wealth inside you; that is where you will find lasting peace, for the body is the abode of God. Therefore, abandoning all outer, sensual pursuits, you should take care of this body-temple. Gurudev exhorts you to rise above all petty things like jealousy, greed, gossip, fault-finding, and bad company, which are the cause of all unhappiness and evil, and to cultivate the good qualities like detachment, desirelessness, contentment, and stillness of mind that bring divine bliss. He advises you to cast off the arrogance of wealth, power, and title and to utilize the rare good fortune of human birth to do pure and noble deeds, to live with morality and righteousness, which brings all happiness.

Gurudev tells you to love all, as everyone is divine, belonging to the one family of God — God who is beyond all religious controversies and caste distinctions. No one is small, impure, or evil. Gurudev says, See with the eye of equality, because God is everywhere and in everyone. He is the One behind the many.

The world is the play of the Self, of Chiti Shakti, of Kundalini, which when awakened in you reveals God in the manifold names and forms of the world. Thus true knowledge lies within. All books and learning are within.

To attain that knowledge you need not renounce the outer world, but you must live in the state of surrender, leaving the outer world as it is and doing continous *japa* to hear the inner mantra. Gurudev tells you to dive within and explore the inner world of lights and the Blue Pearl that dwells in *sahasrāra*. Gurudev sings its glories:

> From there, there is no return.
> It is the land of no weeping,
> the home of prosperity.

Preface to the First Edition

> Muktananda, that is the blue light
> of eternal Consciousness.   [v. 928]

This knowledge cuts asunder your bondage.

All this can be achieved in Ganeshpuri, the abode of *Yogashakti*, the *Siddhaloka* of the earth, if you live there respecting one another.

At the end, Gurudev gives his unique message: This knowledge, this realization, can be easily achieved at the feet of the Guru. When the Guru is pleased and satisfied, all deities give their blessings and all mantras yield their fruits. Gurudev underlines this truth by giving his own experience:

> How glad of heart I am.
> How much I laugh and dance and leap.
> I am immersed in the drunkenness
> of transcendental joy.
> When Nityananda revealed himself
> in my heart,
> I attained this state.   [v. 1008]

Let *Mukteshwari* also be the Guru's grace for us, bringing the intoxication of that same transcendental joy, "the bliss of freedom" — *mukta-ānanda*.

Swami Prajnananda
Gurudev Siddha Peeth
Ganeshpuri, India

For many years, Swami Prajnananda served Swami Muktananda, taking notes of his conversations with the ashramites and visitors, and documenting the meditation experiences people shared after receiving shaktipat. *She wrote* Search for the Self, *the first biography of Swami Muktananda, and was in many ways the first historian of Siddha Yoga, leaving a rich legacy of vividly detailed descriptions of Baba and life in the early days of Gurudev Siddha Peeth.*

Dedication

He who is the supreme fortune
of the entire animate and inanimate
universe of consciousness
from Sadashiva to the earth,
who released for mortal man
the flow of grace of Siddha Mahayoga
in the form of Sri Shiva Shaktipat,
who taught the lesson of oneness
in this world of duality,
transmitting the experience
of the undifferentiated in differences,
who transmuted the world of death
into the world of immortality and truth,
by whose look of grace I lived for ages
and ages and attained the immortal state,
That, my worshipful Gurudeva, is
Existence, Consciousness, and Bliss.
He who is my supreme object of worship,
who is worthy of being remembered every morning,
and of whose grace this Word is
the vibration, to the sacred feet of that
Gurudeva, to divine Nityananda,
this work is dedicated.

स्वामी मुक्तानंद

॥ श्रीगुरुदेव ॥

ब्रह्मवादी जिसे अनुभवयुक्त सिद्धान्तसे "सर्व खल्विदं ब्रह्म" कहते हैं, मुक्तेश्वरी भक्तगण जिस जगतको "सर्वं वासुदेवमिति" कहते हैं, जडवादी जिसे निसर्ग और कारणवादी कारण कहते हैं, वैसे ही मुक्तानंद इस जड चेतनात्मक जगत को "नित्यानंद" कहते हैं ।

वैष्णव विष्णु भक्तिके बिना जीवन रसहीन मानते हैं, शैव शिव पूजाके बिना जीवनको शुष्क कहते हैं, वेदान्ती ब्रह्मानंदके बिना जीवन मृतक-तुल्य जानते हैं, ऐसे ही मुक्तानंद गुरु प्रेमबिना जगत में जीना मौत समझते हैं ।—

जगत में नाम हूँ, बैंकमें खूब पैसा हो, संसारमें कीर्ति हो, सारी बाह्य सम्पदाएँ हों भुक्तानंद गुरु ज्ञान सम्पदाके बिना मनुष्य कंगाल है ।

संसारमें अगर कोई राजा हो, बडा विजयी हो, सत्तावान हो, आस-पास नौकर-चाकर हों, घरमें हाथी-घोडे बंधे हों तो भी मुक्तानन्द गुरु प्रेमामृत की भक्ती बिना वह मृतक है ।

भाषाएँ तो बहुत सी आती हैं, देश तो अनेक देखें हैं, डिग्री भी अनेक पायीं, पैसा की भी कमी नहीं, मुक्तानन्दा आत्मानन्द की कमीसे वह फिर भी भिखारी है ।

जैसे शैवोंके शिव, वैरागियोंके राम, वैष्णवोंके विष्णु, सौरोंके सूर्य और शाक्तोंकी शक्ति है वैसे ही मुक्तानन्द के तो वे गुरु — श्री नित्यानंद हैं ।

Reproduction of a handwritten page of Mukteshwari *from Swami Muktananda's original manuscript.*

I. All Is Nityananda

All Is Nityananda

1. From their own experience,
   knowers of the Self say,
   "All this is indeed Brahman."
   Those whose path is devotion say,
   "All is Vasudeva."
   Those who recognize no conscious creator say,
   "All is nature."
   Those who see God as cause say,
   "The whole world is effect."
   And of this universe,
   both conscious and inert,
   Muktananda says:
   "All is Nityananda."

2. For Vaishnavas
   life is joyless
   without devotion to Vishnu;
   for Shaivas
   it is empty
   without devotion to Shiva;
   for Vedantins
   it is meaningless
   without the bliss of Brahman.
   For Muktananda
   life in this world is like death
   without love for the Guru.

All Is Nityananda

3. You may have fame, money, recognition,
   all the external glories,
   but Muktananda,
   without the wealth of knowledge from the Guru,
   you are destitute.

4. You may be a king,
   triumphant and powerful,
   waited upon by attendants,
   possessing horses and elephants.
   Yet Muktananda, you are no better than dead,
   without the nectar of love for the Guru.

5. As Shiva to Shaivites,
   Rama to Vairagis,
   Vishnu to Vaishnavas,
   the sun to Suryas,
   Shakti to Shaktas,
   so is Nityananda to Muktananda—
   his only Master.

6. As the Void to Buddhists,
   prema to bhaktas,
   the Almighty to those who pray,
   nirvikalpa samadhi to yogis,
   Consciousness to jnanis,
   so is Nityananda to Muktananda.

7. Muktananda searched in the east,
   in the west, in the south, in the north.
   When he came to Ganeshpuri,
   he found Him in his heart.

8. As a Vedantin
   Muktananda filtered subtleties,
   as a bhakta
   he worshiped a chosen deity
   and chanted hymns,
   as a yogi he counted breaths
   and sought truth in action.
   Finally he gave all this up.
   When he became still
   he saw Him in himself
   as "I am He."

All Is Nityananda

9. While I had not seen Him within me,
   Ayodhya was without Rama,
   Gokul and Dwaraka without Krishna,
   Badrinath without Narayana,
   Calcutta without Mother Kali,
   Vrindavan without the Son of Nanda,
   Kashi without Shiva,
   Rameshwar without Mahadeva,
   and Girnar without Guru Datta.
   When I realized Nityananda within me,
   I saw Him in all of them:
   Gokul was full of Krishna,
   Kashi full of Shiva.
   I saw the Self moving through all places.

10. While there was death within me,
    the whole world was subject to death.
    I mistook the unreal for the real.
    But when bliss arose from within,
    I saw immortality sporting even in death.
    Through Nityananda's grace,
    death was no longer death.

11. For a long time
    I did japa of the mahamantra.
    I held anusthans.
    I endured the heat of all that repetition.
    Doing so much japa and tapa
    I almost burnt myself up.
    I lost interest in living.
    But when the compassionate Guru
    sang the note of *So'ham*,
    the inner eternal japa,
    my heart rested in Nityananda.
    The weight of all japas and tapas fell away.

12. Many said, "He is in the heart."
    Yogis told me I would find Him in meditation.
    Others said, "He is in the space
    between the eyebrows."
    Some people encouraged me
    to make arduous pilgrimages,
    and yet others involved me in hatha yoga.
    But when I received the grace of Nityananda,
    I worshiped Him as my own inner Self.

All Is Nityananda

13. I worshiped Shaligram with tulsi leaves.
    I worshiped Shivalinga with bilva leaves.
    I worshiped idols with rituals and
    performed many pujas with hymns and
        mantras.
    It was only wasted time.
    When I saw the luminous divine worship
    in my own heart,
    I obtained the reward of all worship.

14. I continually did japa
    of the five-syllable mantra
    Namah Shivaya with *Om*.
    A long time passed in this way.
    When Nityananda made me repeat *So'ham*,
    japa came of its own accord.
    The external japa fell away.
    I realized that japa occurs by itself
    and just to listen is best.

15. Sri Gurudeva gave me the two syllables:
    I would repeat only them,
    meditate only on them,
    saying *So* while inhaling, *ham* while exhaling.
    As I repeated *So'ham*, I forgot other mantras;
    I attained peace.

All Is Nityananda

16.   I wandered ceaselessly
since childhood, always alone.
I went to many places
and met many great beings.
Still I wandered on.
I came to Ganeshpuri
and met Nityananda.
He stopped my wandering—
and with this the wandering of many.

17.   I saw all kinds of things;
I accepted some and rejected others.
When Guru Nityananda showed me
the underlying truth,
I saw that the accepted and the rejected
were one.

18.   I wandered throughout India
searching continuously for my Gurudev.
I ate mud when I had no food.
I used a dargah sheet when I had no cover.
But I did not lose courage.
As a result, Annapurna, bringing Her treasures
of clothes, food, and wealth,
came to live in me.

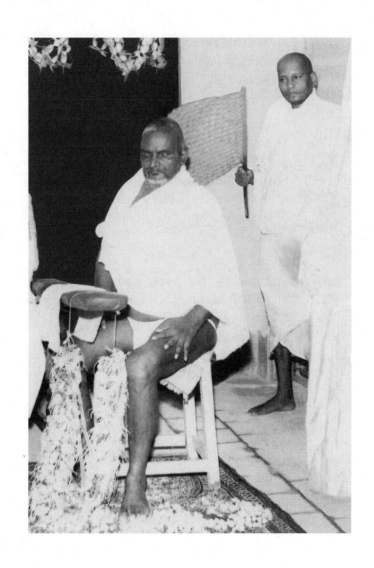

All Is Nityananda

19. Muktananda rested in Nityananda
    and all the fatigue of his spiritual journey
    melted away.

20. The scriptures composed by great seers
    are all undeniably true.
    But you, Muktananda,
    need only read the teachings
    of your own Guru, Sri Nityananda.

21. Muktananda, tread your path resolutely.
    There will be many obstacles and difficulties.
    All sorts of people will try to make you
    like themselves,
    and try to lead you astray.
    Don't listen to any of them.
    Don't ever forget Nityananda.

22. The One who is experienced
    in the innermost recess of the heart lotus
    is called "turiya."
    He is supreme Bliss
    and supreme Consciousness.
    He, truly, is God,
    is Nityananda, is Muktananda.

II. INNER SELF

You Yourself Are What You Seek

23. The inner country
is far more subtle and delightful
than the outer country.
Muktananda, don't wander outside.
Live in the inner world.

24. You yourself are what you seek.
Look inward.
Muktananda, here man becomes civilized.

25. The inner loka is mahaloka.
Explore that world.
The outer world is ordinary.

26. Why would anyone wander fruitlessly,
leaving the temple of the heart,
the mala of the mind,
the japa of *So'ham*, and
the yajna of meditation?

You Yourself Are What You Seek

27. Muktananda,
who would wander from forest to forest
when the divine flame shines in the heart?

28. Muktananda,
why abandon the crystal blue rays
sparkling and smiling in the heart?
Why forsake that wealth of beauty?
Why become a beggar?

29. Kings and beggars,
young and old,
wander outside.
Everyone worships the external.
The man who seeks within is rare.
He alone can be called a man.

30. Muktananda,
bend toward the heart's vibrations
where the playful breeze of Chiti blows.

31. Behold the splendors of the six chakras.
    Behold the gods and goddesses in them.
    Behold the shakti of the seed letters.
    Muktananda, they are your wealth.
    Why beg for external things?

32. Muktananda, all things are within you.
    Receive from within.

33. The great light in the space of the forehead
    is brighter than the sun.
    Muktananda, bow to the inner sun.

34. Muktananda,
    that which is beyond all beyonds
    is supreme Light, is God.
    He is only in the heart.
    He is not outside.

35. The thumb-sized flame
shines in the center of the heart.
By its brightness the world is bright.
Muktananda,
when that is in the heart,
so close,
why do you think it is far?

36. Within the heart lies supreme affection,
boundless enthusiasm, lasting peace,
compassion like nectar.
Muktananda, go there.

37. You forgot your Self and loved others.
You forgot your Self and became lost.
Muktananda, look at your Self.
Nityananda is within.

38. Muktananda,
rest in the intoxication of your own Self.
Your being is saturated with Nityananda.
Do not listen to others.
Inner experience is the only perfect judge.

INNER SELF

39. In the inner Self
there is infinite inspiration.
Open your heart and see.
Man cannot be judged from the outside.

40. What joy can you find in others
if there is none in you?
To seek joy in others will weaken you.
Muktananda, do not listen to others.
Listen to your own bliss.

41. Can a dog know
the intoxication of an elephant?
Let him bark.
Muktananda, rest in your own bliss.
Why should an elephant become a dog?

42. Find contentment in your Self.
Find peace in your Self.
Love your Self.
Muktananda, of what use to you
is the contentment of another?

You Yourself Are What You Seek

43. You are within yourself,
    you are within all.
    Without you, nothing is.
    Muktananda, remain absorbed
    in your inner state.

44. Remain absorbed within.
    Friends will come and go.
    With the figure one you can make a million.
    Without it there is nothing.

45. Your time was wasted meeting others,
    for they could not give you love.
    Muktananda, love will come
    only when you meet your Self.

46. You spent so long taking others for darshan
    and giving darshan yourself.
    You did not see your Self in meditation.
    Muktananda, seeing the Self
    brings the highest peace.

INNER SELF

47. Man's understanding is amazing.
He has the power of discrimination,
yet he does not meditate on the Self
but on all that is other.

48. Be your only friend in the world.
Within your Self
you are your own husband and wife,
son and daughter.
Bliss comes only from the Self.

49. Husband or wife,
daughter or son—
O Muktananda,
how can another be yours?

50. When you are your own husband,
your own wife,
your own daughter and son,
when you find your Self within yourself
you will become immortal.

You Yourself Are What You Seek

51. If you want sublime intoxication,
inner rapture,
first become your own beloved.
Muktananda, when love springs up within,
everything outside is Nityananda.

52. If you want to eat, eat.
If you want to drink, drink.
Work out all your karma.
Muktananda, knowing the Self
to be unattached, absolutely pure,
remain immersed in your own bliss.

53. Sing joyfully, eat joyfully, drink joyfully.
Embrace everyone. Become everyone's.
Meditate on your Self.
Only you are in everything.
Muktananda, what is other than you?

54. Fulfillment is the same
in the world or beyond it,
through the senses or beyond them.
Why then can't you find it in your Self?

55. Muktananda, the visions of the scriptures,
the knowledge of the enlightened,
the consummation of all spiritual disciplines,
are inside you in their completeness.

56. Learning, debating,
verse-making, word play,
are all addictions.
Give them up, Muktananda.
Revel unceasingly
in the pure vibrations of the Self.

57. Because of your existence,
Creation exists.
If you do not exist,
nothing exists.
Muktananda, first know your Self.

58. The world is because you are.
Rama is because you are.
Shiva and Shakti are because you are.
Muktananda, what is, if you are not?

You Yourself Are What You Seek

59. Muktananda,
when you find your Self within
you will see that the world exists
because you exist.
Then you will understand
that the only worthwhile effort
is toward Self-realization.

60. Creation is because I am.
Without 'I' there is nothing.
I am foremost in everything.
Muktananda, *aham brahmasmi*,
"I am Brahman."

61. What are you looking for
east and west,
north and south,
above and below?
Muktananda, the whole universe
you alone are, you alone are,
you alone are.

Inner Self

62. Rama, Sri Krishna, Shiva, Sri Durga,
    Ganesha, Dinesha, Jnanesha—
    O Muktananda,
    you alone, you alone, you alone.

63. Badri, Kedar, Kashi, Rameshwar,
    Dwaraka, Rishikesh, Sriranga,
    and holy Mathura—O Muktananda,
    only you, only you, only you.

64. The Ganges, the Yamuna,
    the Saraswati, the Narmada,
    the Sindhu, the Alaknanda, the Kapila,
    holy Pushkar and Kashi—
    all these, Muktananda,
    in you, in you, in you.

You Yourself Are What You Seek

65. Wherever you go
     you will find only your Self.
     In Ayodhya you are the Rama
     who pervades everything.
     In Gokul you are the Krishna
     who enchants.
     In Kashi you are the Shiva
     who performs auspicious deeds.
     You are the Parashiva of Kailas,
     Sri Vishnu of Vaikuntha.
     Muktananda, you are one in all.

The Bliss of the Atman

66. He speaks many languages,
    has seen many countries,
    has attained many degrees,
    has no lack of fame.
    But Muktananda!
    Lacking the bliss of the Atman
    he is still a beggar.

67. A man who has attained full awareness
    of the indwelling, blissful, and conscious Self
    lives in Vaikuntha even while in the body.

68. The all-pervasive God is within you.
    See Him and adore Him.
    Through realizing Him,
    your life will unfold in all its perfection.
    You will no longer weep.

The Bliss of the Atman

69. Parashiva is everywhere.
    The distinctions between man and man,
    between belief and belief,
    and the distinctions created by logic
    are all illusory.
    Muktananda, keep away from them.
    Go and sit within yourself.

70. In my search for Him I traveled far,
    traveled wide, questioned many.
    No answer appeared. When I returned
    I saw Him within my own Self.

71. I worshiped gods and goddesses,
    made pilgrimages, vows, performed yajnas,
    did japa and anushthanas.
    They only wearied me.
    When I knew my Self,
    perfect peace came into my heart.

INNER SELF

72. Beloved people,
    where are you trying to go,
    wandering first here and then there?
    Turn around!
    You will experience within yourself
    complete nectarean bliss.

73. Do not go forward, do not turn back;
    do not look up, do not rush down.
    Wherever you are,
    whatever your condition,
    just rest in your inner Self
    and enjoy its happiness.

74. Brothers, find internal wealth.
    It is truly priceless.
    Thieves can't get at it,
    the government can't tax it —
    only you will enjoy it.

The Bliss of the Atman

75. Do japa and tapa and yoga,
    be a bhakta, sing the praises of the Lord,
    perform yajnas, give in charity,
    be a renunciant or become attached,
    but don't forget the inner Self.
    Muktananda, in all things
    the Self is foremost.

76. Free from the idea of duality,
    from the mutations of the external world,
    free from anxiety
    about what you have or have not attained,
    maintain a steady absorption in Brahman—
    Muktananda, this is the highest realization.

77. Vaikuntha, Goloka, Devaloka, Kailas,
    and the transcendental land of the yogis
    are all in the sahasrara.
    It is here that you must dwell.

78. Muktananda, go to the land
where the most divine melodies resound,
where truly delicious nectar flows,
where the cool and tender light shines,
where brilliant light blazes
with the radiance of a million suns,
where jnanis, bhaktas, yogis,
and lovers of mankind
all live blissfully. What can you get
from this dreary world?

79. Muktananda, your true place is in the center
of the divine effulgence in the sahasrara,
in the midst of that cool,
gentle, and blissful pool of gladness
where bells, kettledrums, flutes,
and the transcendental music resound
in the shimmering rays of pure Consciousness.

80. Lakes, rivers, and oceans are separate,
but water is the same in all.
There are many mountain ranges,
but their earth is the same.
In all the different clouds,
the drops of water are the same.
In many bodies, the Self is one.

The Bliss of the Atman

81. In all logs, fire is the same;
in all pots, clay is the same;
in all threads and fibers,
cotton is the same.
The same Self pervades the whole universe.

82. As oil is the same in all sesame seeds,
fire in all logs,
and butter in all milk,
the Self is the same in all bodies.

83. Muktananda, go beyond distinctions
of caste, race, nation.
They are imaginary.
Become absorbed in the pure Self.

The Self Reveals the Self

84. The Self is perfect.
    The Self is immutable.
    That pervades the animate
    and the inanimate.
    Nothing can make It change.

85. What will That eat?
    What will That drink?
    What will That enjoy?
    Muktananda,
    the Self is without body or attribute.
    That is pure and perfect.

86. To purify the pure,
    to purge the untainted,
    to seek what one has already—
    Muktananda, isn't that a child's game?

The Self Reveals the Self

87. How can you purify That
which is completely pure?
Why search for That
when it is all-pervading?
Where will you see That
which is always within you?
Muktananda, know that your Self
fills all creation.
Be drunk with bliss.

88. How can That be a householder?
How a sannyasin?
What is the meaning of man and woman,
who are but puppets of the five elements?
The Self is separate from everything.
It is the great witness,
completely full, completely pure.
Muktananda, know this
and be drunk with bliss.

89. You see the sun by its own light,
and the moonlight too.
The luster of the stars reveals the stars.
Muktananda, the ecstatic bliss of the Self
reveals the Self.

90. Free from mine and thine,
free from caste and individuality,
free from duality and non-duality,
vibrating with bliss—
by this the Self is known.

91. When you see, what else can you see?
When you receive, what else can you receive?
Who else is the giver but the Self?
Muktananda, understand
that the Self is everlasting,
free from thought, completely pure.
Do not dissipate your energies.
Become absorbed in the Self.

III. KUNDALINI

Awakening Chiti Shakti

92. Through love the sun shines.
    By love the moon is cool.
    The clouds shed rain through love.
    Muktananda, by love of the Guru
    Kundalini awakes.

93. Only a doctor is qualified to give medicine,
    a lawyer to practice law,
    a teacher to teach.
    Only a Guru can activate Kundalini.

94. Kundalini is the basis of all yoga-tantras.
    All yogas are attainable
    by the awakening of Kundalini.

95. Muktananda,
    if the all-pervasive Kundalini,
    the basis of all tantras,
    has not yet shown Herself,
    has not yet blessed you,
    should you turn away from the Guru?

Awakening Chiti Shakti

96. The Shakti fills your whole body,
    yet you don't know Her.
    The Chiti who is revealed to the jnanis
    is not revealed within you.
    How then do you dare to call yourself wise?

97. Even Hari and Hara need Her.
    Even Brahma seeks Her help.
    With Her grace yogis become full of joy.
    Aren't those people fools who say,
    "Why should we who live in the world
    need the nectar-bestowing Kundalini?"

98. Kundalini makes the body firm,
    makes the old young,
    and strengthens the bodily constituents
    so that man may find immortality.
    That is Her work.

99. Kundalini bestows the fruit
    of the six purificatory exercises.
    She activates prana-apana.
    She stabilizes kumbhaka
    so that man may become absorbed in the Self.
    That is Her work.

100. Kundalini makes a man perform the four yogas.
She steadies the senses,
makes the mind one-pointed
so that it is filled with bliss.
That is Her work.

101. Kundalini pierces the six chakras,
opens the three knots,
and washes away the three impurities
so that man's consciousness
is lifted above the trikuti.
That is Her work.

102. Kundalini takes you above the three states,
beyond the five sheaths,
beyond the three gunas
to the natural throbbing of Consciousness.
That is Her work.

103. Through Kundalini
you experience the millions of suns
in the sahasrara; you sway in the orbit
of highest Consciousness.
That is Her work.

Awakening Chiti Shakti

104. To make one dwell in one's true nature,
devoid of inside, outside, and middle,
devoid of 'this' or 'that,'
devoid of speech and hearing,
devoid of void—Muktananda,
that is the work of Kundalini.

105. Kundalini has the form of *Om*.
She is the giver of perfect bliss.
She is both male and female.
She is the all-knowing Yogini.
She is the Goddess of yoga.

106. Kundalini is the fire of yoga.
She is the eater of maya,
the protectress of knowledge,
the perfect Goddess.
She accomplishes all inner work.

107. When the coiled Kundalini awakens,
kriyas begin.
Sins and suffering are destroyed.
Bliss is born.

108. When there are inner kriyas, outer kriyas,
the kriyas of raja, hatha, bhakti,
and mantra yoga,
life is filled with joy.

109. When you see the divine light within,
hear the celestial music,
drink the sweet and savory juices,
life becomes filled with nectar.

110. Muktananda,
when by Guru's grace
one knows the love-intoxication of Kundalini,
the merging into Shiva-Shakti,
and the entry into Brahman,
then one knows Self-realization.

111. Kundalini pierces the trikuti
and moves in the sahasrara.

112. Kundalini, Shakti, Gurukripa,
the inner awakening.
Muktananda, all these are synonymous.

Awakening Chiti Shakti

113. Muktananda, the world is filled with Chiti.
People, universe, cosmos are filled with Chiti.
Truly, all is Chiti.

114. Chiti is prana-apana.
She causes the mind to think.
She is the vital force of life.
Muktananda, there is really nothing but Chiti.

115. Kundalini, the universal Mother,
encompasses all yogas.
She is the form and essence of the mantra.
When you receive the mantra
through the Guru's grace,
She is quickly awakened.

116. The awakening of Kundalini—
whose form is the mantra—
and Her rejoicing
are one and the same.

117. Mantra, Guru, Kundalini, and Chiti
are all the playful Shakti
of the same God.

Play of Chiti Shakti

118. Kundalini Shakti
is the prana of the universe.
By the power of this great Goddess
the universe exists.
Muktananda, know Her.

119. This world is the play of Chiti Shakti.
Chiti appears in the form of the world.
Muktananda, accept Her as your deity.

120. Only one who is evil
will see the world as evil.
It is the play of Chiti,
imbued with divine power.

121. Cloth is nothing but thread,
ornaments nothing but gold.
God is the world.
To perceive two is sin.
There is only Chiti's play.

Play of Chiti Shakti

122. Ornaments are gold through and through.
Muktananda, you are filled with Chiti.
See only Chiti within and without.

123. Earrings and bracelets are made of gold,
dhotis and saris of cotton,
pots and pitchers of clay;
so it is with man and woman
who are both of the Goddess Chiti.

124. The same Consciousness is in man and woman.
Muktananda, give up distinction.
In Consciousness there cannot be two.

125. Shiva is Shakti.
Shiva manifests through Shakti.
When the inner Shakti awakens,
Muktananda, they are again indistinguishable.

126. Chiti is Lakshmi.
She is Saraswati and Kali.
The cosmos is pervaded by Her.
Muktananda, the Chiti without
is Kundalini within.

127. When Kundalini awakes,
all doors are thrown open.
Rama reveals Himself in the heart.
Muktananda, love Kundalini.

128. When Kundalini awakes,
the eyes are filled with light,
fragrance rises,
nectar bathes the tongue,
ecstasy plays in the heart.

129. Taste returns to food,
poverty flees,
youth comes to old age.
Muktananda,
Kundalini is the power of Will,
the maiden Uma.

130. You can see distant places,
speech becomes powerful,
the music of God resounds within.
Muktananda, worship Kundalini.

131. When Kundalini wakens the limbs
you dance, *ta thai! ta thai!*
Inspiration rushes and bounds
through the blood.
Muktananda, this is the ecstasy
of self-forgetfulness.

132. Inside, the lights sparkle and shine—
blue, yellow, white.
Inside, divine music plays—
veena, kettledrum, tabor.
Muktananda, this is the mahaprasad
of Guru's grace, of Kundalini.

IV. Yoga and Worldly Life

Value of Human Birth

133. Muktananda, human birth is rare
and time very precious.
Make the best use of your time.
Meditate on your Self.

134. The body you have obtained
is extremely precious.
You may not get another.
Muktananda,
live by the sweat of your brow.
Do not live off others.

135. Dependence on others is misery,
even when it feels pleasant.
Only independence is happiness.

136. A life lived by one's own labor
is a sweet delicacy.
It contains all realizations.
Muktananda, live like this.

Giving and Receiving

137. *B*e hesitant in taking, sure in giving.
Perform the yajna of doing your own work.
Muktananda, how far is heaven then?

138. Muktananda, give of yourself to others.
Do not always take.
In giving your merit increases.
In taking it decreases.

139. You receive because you give.
If you do not give, how will you receive?
Muktananda, do not mislead others.
You cannot just receive.

140. Everyone gives and takes
according to his nature.
So why weep, blaming others?
Muktananda,
when you give with reverence
you receive with reverence.

141. Men may drink and drink
but the Ganges will always be full.
Muktananda, drink as much as you want.
Don't resent what others take
when you yourself do nothing.

142. The food and water that you take
pass out through the other end.
If you are rich, give a little in charity.
Only what you give will remain with you.

143. Giving is in harmony with God's will.
It is a shining act of love.
Give liberally, as God gives.

144. Always give freely, withholding nothing.
You will reach God.
A farmer understands the importance of giving.
For the little he gives to the earth,
he receives abundantly in return.

145. Give freely, as God gives.
If, after giving, you forget about it,
then that gift grows fully.

Status, Wealth, and Power

146. On the bright days
of your brief life
remain aware.
Live with morality and righteousness.
Power will go one day.

147. Do not make others suffer
through pride of power.
Muktananda, save yourself from this sin.

148. Power comes from others.
If you regard it as your own
and inflict suffering,
think what your condition will be,
Muktananda, after you lose it.

149. Arrogance of wealth, family, power,
degree or title—
Muktananda, who will be your companion
when you have lost everything?

Yoga and Worldly Life

150. Power and status are a nine-day wonder.
Who will stand by you
when they are gone?

151. Those who salute you
while you hold power,
will ignore you when you lose it.

152. Muktananda, look at the plight
of fallen leaders.
Carry yourself without arrogance.

153. The world changes, power changes,
likewise the preoccupations of man.
Muktananda, do not get too attached
to status.
It will not last.

154. You claim to be rich without riches.
You pretend to be virtuous without virtues.
Your cleverness is without culture.
Muktananda, what's the use?

Status, Wealth, and Power

155. There are men who wield power
without pride,
who are rich but simple in their ways,
who are learned but have no arrogance.
They are divine spirits in human form.

156. The infinite Spirit witnesses
the varied universe.
It sees that endless structure
and never tires.
You watch your little wealth.
Why does that exhaust you
and burn up your heart?

157. Much time has gone in conceits of wealth,
family, and status.
These are impediments.
Muktananda, be full of renunciation.
Meditate.
You will find happiness.

158. Shyam lives in all hearts.
He dwells in steadiness and patience.
Man, do not be arrogant.

159. Muktananda, the Lord who dwells within
is all-knowing.
He watches your actions.
He must spend His days repenting
because of what you do.

160. Satisfy the indwelling God.
The gift of peace comes from within.
Unless God has blessed you, Muktananda,
how will you sleep in joy?

161. Man, your arrogance is futile.
Nobility of heart is priceless.
Cultivate it.

162. Power and position
reside in the noble human form
but they are only adjuncts.
Muktananda, do not forget the Self.

163. Muktananda, give up talking nonsense.
Give up running after people.
Earn inner wealth.

Status, Wealth, and Power

164. Man, in your innermost nature
you are simple, unpretentious, and noble.
When you are drunk with power
you insult your Self.
Status and power are nothing
compared to inner worth.

165. As the Self you are completely pure.
Just as impurity is imagined to exist
in the Self,
so power is illusory
with respect to humanity.

166. Life is hardly a day.
Death hovers, counting the minutes.
Think about life's journey, Muktananda.
Give up conceit.
Explore the path of peace.

167. Manners, riches, caste, and power
are man-made wealth.
They count only in this world.
Muktananda, God is bought with love alone.

Speech

168. Speak words that are sweet,
agreeable, and beneficial.
Muktananda,
what is the need of mantra repetition
for one who always speaks sweet words?

169. When pleasant words,
sweet delivery, and spiritual theme
are united with joy,
they become holy singing.

The Human Body

170. You obtained your body by God's grace.
     It is a precious gift and deserves right use.
     Use it for meditation.
     You will drink the nectar of immortality.

171. Revere the body and care for it,
     for it is a temple.
     In it the perfect blue god dwells.
     Muktananda has attained God in this very body.

172. There is one who lives in the body,
     who pervades it and knows it
     through and through.
     Muktananda, that inner Knower
     is your nature.

173. The seer of the waking world,
     the seer of the dream world,
     the enjoyer of bliss—
     that is your inner Self.

Yoga and Worldly Life

174. He is not the body but lives in it.
He is not the senses but lives in them.
He is the source of inner knowledge.
That God of gods is Mahadeva.

175. In the mud of a pond, a lotus.
In the pollen of a flower, honey.
In the navel of a deer, musk.
In the body, God.

176. The body is God's abode.
Don't become a beast
that only eats and drinks.

177. As threads make up cloth,
Chiti Kundalini permeates the body.
Muktananda, keep the body pure.

178. Your body is made of five elements.
It can be big or small, young or old,
but the Self within is ageless and deathless.

The Human Body

179. Boys and girls,
you may be young but you are not small.
Your future greatness is already within you.

180. As children are quick to learn,
so they are open to meditation.

181. How can you be insignificant?
Your body has the greatness
of the primal elements.
How can you be a child?
The soul within you has no beginning.

182. The world is made of five elements,
and so is your body.
Experience this unity.

183. The body consists of 72 million nadis.
Understand its value.
Seek out its treasures.
There is no time to lose.

184. In the center of the 72 million nadis
there is the central nadi.
Muktananda,
that is the dwelling place of the Most High.

185. Sushumna is the central nadi.
It blazes with a golden light.
In the center of that light
saints sleep joyfully.
Muktananda, go there.

186. Behold sushumna's glory.
See her ways and laws.
In that high place
worlds are made and worlds dissolve.
Muktananda, look there
where the Beholder revels in the Self.

187. The human body is the true temple.
Have no anxiety, have no doubt.
The Lord of the Self lives there.
Muktananda, enter within and see.

Food

188. From the nectar of food
that comes from the abundant earth,
you are born.
By eating food, your life is sustained.
Always love the body
that is made of food.
In the end food merges into food.

189. Food is Brahman.
Take it like medicine.
Take it as prasad.
Then food will be transformed into nectar
and will nourish you.

190. As you take medicine in a measured dose,
take food in a measured, frugal quantity.
Eat with restraint and reverence — to live.
Food is your heaven.

Food

191. Eat with love and contentment—
to live and to acquire strength.
Don't live to eat.
Perceive food as Brahman.

192. As health, strength, fame,
enthusiasm, and inspiration
come from regular eating,
irregular eating destroys these things.

193. To eat food understanding its importance,
to live in the awareness of the inner Self,
to live with discipline,
to restrain the senses—
this is the religion of man.

Love

194. Disparaging the world
is like washing yourself
in dirty water.
Bathe only in the nectar of love
that fills the inner spaces.
It is as sweet as the elixir of immortality
and makes the soul tremble with gladness.

195. Make love your life.
Make love your deity.
Become a love-addict.
Muktananda, if you can live without love
you are not human.

196. Love all as yourself.
Be completely without desire.
Muktananda, love without desire
is true worship.

Love

197. Love is man's greatest wealth.
In the form of love
God dwells in man.
Love is the nature of the Guru.
Love is a great quality,
and worthy of reverence.

198. Let your love for God grow every day,
and let that love be without motive.
Muktananda, love is the herb of immortality.

199. Love is the image of Narayana,
love is the true nature of the Self,
love is worship, love is arati.
Without love, religious observances are lifeless.

200. Out of love the universe unfolds.
Love is Rama, love is Krishna.
Muktananda, the pure selfless love
of the senses, free of desire,
is Nityananda.

Yoga and Worldly Life

201. You can do japa,
 practice austerities, meditation, and yoga,
 perform the rituals prescribed in the scriptures,
 make praiseworthy efforts of every kind,
 make wonderful speeches—
 but without love all this is nothing.

202. Nothing in the world
 is higher than love.
 Love is the wealth of the heart.

203. Love turns an enemy into a friend.
 Love frees a serpent of its poison.
 Love conquers the supreme Lord.
 Muktananda, love is the projection of the Self.

204. Love is the inner, the universal,
 the cosmic Self.
 Love is realization.
 Without love,
 all sadhanas are just hard labor.

Love

205. Out of love
the earth brings forth nectarean food.
Out of love
seasons change.
Out of love
the wind blows tirelessly.
Out of love
the good are worshiped.
Muktananda,
love is the revelation of God.

Loyalty

206. One wife, one husband, one mantra,
one Guru, one divine Name,
and a one-pointed mind—
Muktananda, this is true fidelity.

207. Worship of all sorts of gurus and deities,
pledges of loyalty to many women—
Muktananda, these are the holy rites
of a depraved man.

208. The pledge of fidelity to one woman,
unswerving devotion to one's country,
deference to the venerable old—
Muktananda, these are the marks
of a man of quality.

209. A man without single-minded devotion,
without delight in good deeds,
without faith in God,
who is a slave of many women—
Muktananda, is he not an inmate
of the house for worthless bulls?

Loyalty

210. If a man is not loyal to his wife,
if he does not have affection for her,
Muktananda, his depravity will lead him to hell.

211. Fidelity to one woman is a great pledge
and a great initiation.
It brings one to the land of peace.
The man who vows loyalty to his wife is ideal.

212. A woman who is not simple and restrained,
who does not love her husband as herself—
Muktananda, is she not a wild bear?

213. The woman who lives in her husband
is a supreme deity.
She is everything to him—
mother, friend, secretary,
servant, wellwisher.
To remember her every morning
is to remember the Divine.

214. The true woman's surrender is complete.
She thus becomes one with her husband
and lives like a jewel in the family.
She is a place of pilgrimage,
Mahashakti, Goddess Chiti Kundalini,
the universal Mother.

215. A wife whose every action
expresses perfect devotion to her husband,
who is faithful to her vows,
loyal and saintly in her heart,
who is skillful in practical life,
strong-minded, full of forgiveness—
Muktananda, even God desires
the darshan of such a one!

216. The woman who sees her husband as God
and her work as a sacrifice to God,
who lives in harmony with her neighbors
and becomes the mother-Guru
to her sons and daughters—
Muktananda,
she is a sacred place of pilgrimage.

Dharma

217. Life in this mutable world
lasts only a few days.
Muktananda, the true man works
for the happiness and welfare
of his fellow men.

218. A life filled with work,
contentment in what you have,
a strong sense of duty—
these are the gates to the temple of peace.

219. Life without dharma
is unworthy of man.
Follow dharma.
Comprehend it.
Dharma is God.

220. To see the one Self in all,
to have a heart that is forgiving,
to live on the fruits of one's own work,
and in the awareness
of each other's divinity—
this is the religion of man.

221. To see the divinity of others
and to let this knowledge guide your actions—
during sadhana and after it—
this is the religion of man.
It is the essence of devotion.
It is the secret of a country's progress
and the best plan for development.

222. While you don't repeat the mantra
"See each other as divine,"
while you retain the mantra
of differences in your heart,
while you are without reverence
and respect for other people,
you cannot find peace, even in a dream.

Dharma

223. In attachment to the senses,
in love bound by the senses,
are the roots of decline.
In love for the boundless Lord,
in absorption in Him,
are heaven and the essence of progress.

224. A heart full of reverence
because one knows that the world
and oneself are one;
affection and reverence for Guru,
mother, and father;
love for one's country—
this is the religion of man.

225. Care of one's own wealth,
detachment from the wealth of others;
love for one's own wife,
respect for the wives of others;
living without duality;
thinking according to Vedanta—
this is the religion of man.

226. This world is born from Manu.
To see the human race as one,
and everyone as human,
and to act accordingly—
this is the religion of man.

227. Loving the Lord,
cultivating virtue,
serving the Guru,
losing oneself in meditation—
Muktananda, these give a man
contentment within himself.

228. Get up early, go to bed early.
Worship the Lord every day.
Honor your father and mother.
This life will bring you happiness.

229. Let your deeds be pure
and your thoughts noble.
Practice self-restraint.
Be absorbed in meditation.
Then see how all the gods
will make you their dwelling place.

Dharma

230. You may be a king or a lord of wealth.
You may have the eight great siddhis
in your pocket.
Muktananda, without purity
there is no peace.

231. Be pure in mind, in speech, in deed.
Purity alone is the mother of peace.
The joy in the heart of a man without sin
is reflected in his face.

232. Grow your crops with love,
do that for Rama.
Do business fairly,
that for Shyam.
In politics, remember God.
Muktananda, there is no peace
without the Lord.

233. From one man's peace
many receive peace.
Could discontentment
ever be the gift of Nityananda?
Muktananda, earn peace in your heart.

234. The worship of living Consciousness
bears fruit at once.
Muktananda, worship conscious beings.
You will find peace.

235. You owe your birth
to your mother and father.
Lovingly do what they ask of you.
Muktananda, by worshiping your parents
you will find peace.

236. Muktananda,
in honoring father and mother,
the Guru and the old,
you worship God.

237. A mind that is silent and still,
a life free from debt,
selfless service to the Guru —
Muktananda, Vaikuntha is in these,
not far away.

Dharma

238. Learn to sit in a natural manner.
Learn to be steady, calm, detached.
As you learn to sit still,
as you cease to react,
your mind will also become steady.

239. To live on the fruits of your own effort,
to get on with your own work,
to be calm and not to disturb others—
this is a great yajna.

240. Only noble qualities,
sattvic food, and a pure mind
will give you inner peace.

241. Unnecessary talking,
undisciplined eating and sleeping,
wasteful discarding of semen—
Muktananda, discarding of feces is better.

242. Staying up at night for no reason,
sleeping unnecessarily in the day,
eating irregularly—
Muktananda, the reward of this discipline
is the misery of hell.

243. Chant with love.
Meditate with love.
Remember the Lord with love.

244. Always contemplate Him within
even while going about your daily tasks.
This, Muktananda, is jnana, bhakti,
love, and yoga.

Adharma

245. If a race is to be destroyed,
be sure there need be no other cause
than the corruption of its women.

246. When man destroys the dharma of woman
the world is filled with sinfulness.
Bombs don't have to be dropped on that nation.

247. When women are degraded,
the nation becomes degraded.
When women become corrupt,
the world is destroyed.
Muktananda, never go
where women are not pure.

248. The mother's place in the world is high.
The Upanishads say,
"Consider the mother divine."
To him who serves his mother,
God is revealed.

249. Don't speak ill of woman.
Don't look at her with sin in your eye.
By pure devotion to woman
you will find supreme bliss.

250. You were born in the womb of woman.
You grew sucking her breast.
O Muktananda, why do you destroy yourself
by constantly accusing her?

251. Women have been great yoginis,
great queens, faithful wives.
Muktananda, honor woman.

252. Man, woman is your birthplace,
not a land of indulgence.
Because of debased understanding,
you have turned heaven into hell.

253. Sita, Savitri, Mandodari, Damayanti,
Tara, Ahalya, Madalasa, Lalli Yogini—
these were exalted women!

Adharma

254. When woman is corrupt, the world falls,
when she is impure, virtue is lost.
Muktananda, such women are the pit of hell.

255. Unwilling to serve her husband,
without affection for her son,
violating the family tradition—
know such a woman to be a scourge.

256. Fond of quarreling, self-willed,
husband of her husband,
indifferent to religion and morality—
Muktananda, know her to be
a pit of hell in a woman's form.

257. If a woman drinks heavily,
is shameless in her dress,
is full of stupid chatter
and always ready for a quarrel,
she is hell on earth.

258. A woman who has not become her husband,
who has not merged with him,
who has never been his true mate,
who has no joy in serving him—
Muktananda, is she not a pestilence?

259. A loyal wife possesses glory.
Her vows are her faith
and she lives for her family.
The gods worship her feet.

260. A woman who does not love her husband
with pure and guileless love,
who has not become one with him,
a woman who turns against her husband,
who is full of wrath and whorish—
Muktananda, isn't a tigress better than she?

261. Muktananda, is there a more horrible hell
than sexual indulgence
with a man other than one's husband
or a woman other than one's wife,
and unceasing pursuit of carnal pleasure?

Adharma

262. Eating, sleeping, fearfulness, sensuality,
are aspects of the temptress Maya.
Mastery of the senses, courage,
dispassionate devotion, love,
are qualities of a true human being.

263. The nation whose people live a life of sensuality
certainly cannot become radiant and victorious.

264. How much humanity can a man have
when he does not have his senses
under control?

265. If you want love, beauty, and respect
in your life,
control your senses.

Divinity Revealed

266. As long as I looked upon woman as woman,
I spent my days in fear.
When I saw her as the Divine Mother
my fear vanished.

267. One is married, another a widow.
One is young, another old.
All are portions of Narayani,
Lakshmi, Saraswati.
All are filled with Chiti.
Muktananda, let your eye be pure.

268. A woman may mother a king or a god.
She may be chaste and loyal as a wife.
But unless she has been touched
by the Goddess Chiti Kundalini,
she is unprotected, an orphan.

Divinity Revealed

269. When Chiti has unfolded Herself
a woman becomes perfect.
Only she can be loyal, chaste like Savitri,
a perfect mother.
To be reborn through her
would bring no pain.

270. She may marry a man of superlative strength.
She may bear a hero or a philanthropist.
But if she cannot turn others
toward meditation, everything is futile.

271. She who has found the inner light
is a goddess who walks on earth.
She is divinity revealed.
Her darshan is sacred.

272. Her beauty is perfect.
She abounds in wealth.
She comes from a good family tradition.
Muktananda, without inner unfolding
that woman is incomplete.

273.   The woman whose Shakti is awakened
is the Ganges, the Yamuna,
the Saraswati, the Kaveri.
The woman who is filled with Chiti
is no different from a goddess.
She is Gauri, Amba, Lakshmi, Saraswati.

The Pure Self in the World

274. As a single drop of curd
will sour a sea of milk,
a single drop of the nectar of Guru's grace
will transform your life here on earth
into a sweet ocean of bliss.

275. Once milk has become curd
it cannot be turned back into milk again;
once a life has been made spiritual
it will not become worldly again.

276. Butter once churned from curd
will not mix with it again;
oil extracted from sesame seeds
cannot become part of them again.
The Self realized through knowledge
will not be obscured by worldly values
though you remain involved in the world.

Yoga and Worldly Life

277. Just as an owl
can never see light during the day,
by Nityananda's grace
you will never see the world as world.

278. As an owl does not see in the day,
as a crow does not see at night,
so one who is established in knowledge
does not see ignorance even in worldly life.

279. Once the pure Self
has become separate from the gross elements,
it never again loses its purity.

v. The World Is as You See It

Divine Eye

280. There are two guiding viewpoints:
that of the Guru which reveals Vaikuntha
and that of sin which finds fault
and brings one to sorrow.
Muktananda, which is yours?

281. Contemplation of Self and God
is divine wealth.
Muktananda, let your viewpoint be divine.

282. There is no heaven like an innocent eye,
no hell like the eye that disparages.
Muktananda, acquire the wealth
of the eye that sees heaven.
Who cares for a pauper?

283. The sins of the organs of perception
are greater than the sins
of the organs of action.
Muktananda, keep your eye pure.

Divine Eye

284. A man's vision creates his world.
Muktananda, Vaikuntha exists in your eye.

285. Distinctions are made in your eye.
Heaven and hell are there.
Muktananda, if you remove the evil
from your eye
you will see heaven even in hell.

286. Man reaps the fruit of his own attitude.
Right attitude is a pilgrimage
to Vaikuntha.

287. Thought creates the world.
Thought determines all actions.
Thoughts of bhakti make a bhakta.
Muktananda, heaven stands
in your own thought.

288. Even in heaven there is no happiness
when Creation is limited by the eye of man.
Muktananda, as your eye merges with Shiva
you will see supreme bliss.

289. Fill your eye with knowledge
 and see the world as Rama.
 The scriptures all teach this.
 What is wrong with your eye, Muktananda,
 that you can only look for differences?

290. The world is as you see it.
 Your attitude creates your subtle karma.
 Muktananda, first reform your attitude.

291. You see the world as world.
 Thus you only see differences.
 Muktananda, fill your eye with Nityananda.

292. The inhabitants of hell
 must suffer its torments.
 For them there is no escape.
 But, Muktananda, why do you suffer hell
 by your habit of seeing hell?

293. The man whose eye has Hari's compassion
 will see heaven even in hell.

Divine Eye

294. In the court of God, all are equal.
Go there and be tranquil.
Muktananda, why do you watch others?
Why do you burn with jealousy?

295. You think success lies in
making others understand.
Muktananda, success lies in
making yourself understand the importance
of seeing purity in impurity.

296. There are men who have qualities
you lack.
There are men with riches
far greater than yours.
Why does that make you languish?
Muktananda, examine your own worth.
What world has your attitude created?

The World Is as You See It

297. Where the world is, Muktananda,
there is illusion.
If you see diversity instead of unity,
world instead of God,
inequalities everywhere,
it is your eye that sins against you.
Cast it out.
See Chiti everywhere.

298. From the eye, seeing.
From seeing, thinking.
From thinking, reflection.
The fruit of reflection
is the food of the mind.
Muktananda, care for your eye.

Faulty Eye

299. Acquire excellence,
cultivate your potential,
increase your purity.
Muktananda,
do not waste your vital self
deprecating others.

300. Do not drink the poison of disparagement.
Do not give up Nityananda's immortal elixir.
Muktananda, why did you forget Nityananda
and think ill of others?

301. Why do you gossip about others, you fool?
Is sin so interesting?
Are you the one who heads the little band
that sits in judgment on the rest?

302. Through lack of intelligence,
wild animals eat offal;
through lack of intelligence,
wild birds drink filth;
and man, who thinks himself intelligent,
feeds on the faults of others.
Muktananda, is this a cleaner habit?

303. A crow delights in carrion.
A cuckoo loves music.
Stinking mire is heaven to a pig.
A drop of rain is the chataka bird's nectar.
There are certain men who differ from the rest;
disparagement of others
is not their source of life.
They are called virtuous.

304. Muktananda, examine your own home,
your family, your world.
Are they above reproach?
Does heaven dwell there?

Faulty Eye

305. To deceive your wife,
to seat malice in your heart,
to cheat your partner—
Muktananda, is this your culture?

306. Look at your sons and daughters,
your own family conduct.
Look behind closed doors.
What is the duty of a respectable man?
To visit the sacred place
of another man's wife?

307. God's justice can be seen
in your actions, in your children.
Muktananda, investigate your own life.
Leave others alone.

308. While you are obsessed with others' faults
you cannot see your own faults
and the lethargy of your ways.
O Muktananda, that is hell on earth.

The World Is as You See It

309. You live in hell,
your friends and relations are from hell,
your ways are the ways of hell.
O Muktananda, you are deep in hell
and yet you disparage the sinless.

310. The agony of a snakebite
or sting of a scorpion
is not so bad.
Burning in fire or drowning in water
is not so bad.
But, beware of a fault-finder,
O Muktananda!
He is without Guru's grace.

311. The wild animal does not calculate,
the wild bird does not think of tomorrow.
The two-legged predator is far more dangerous,
for the suffering he inflicts is deliberate.
Muktananda, keep away from him.

Faulty Eye

312.　An animal kills another
　　　only when tormented by hunger.
　　　Man's violence on man is different.
　　　He attacks for pleasure
　　　and when his stomach is full.

313.　Learned Sir,
　　　deep and joyful rest lies within.
　　　If you must enlighten somebody,
　　　enlighten yourself.
　　　If you must delight in something,
　　　delight in your Self.

314.　While explaining to others their defects
　　　don't let yourself become spoiled.
　　　While reforming those around you
　　　make sure that you remain pure.

315.　Muktananda, do not see, discuss, or write
　　　about the sins of others.
　　　Do not dwell on them.
　　　Live, instead, in the contemplation
　　　of your Self.
　　　This is the heavenly religion of man.

The World Is as You See It

316.   A principled man
does not speak ill of others,
for he knows that to be unforgivable.
When he sees his family suffering,
he repents of past sins.

317.   Man, your destiny
is the witness of your worth,
yet you blame other people.
Is this not sheer stupidity? Fortunately,
there are many wise men in the world
who know the truth.

318.   You may ridicule the virtuous
or twist sin into virtue.
What you do remains with you.
Muktananda, it cannot be concealed,
even if you try.

319.   It does not matter
if the world knows your defects,
but virtues are better concealed.
It is better to be disparaged
than to disparage others.

Faulty Eye

320. Conceal your merits
as you conceal your wealth.
Your defects are obstacles.
Let them be criticized.
Muktananda, don't look for others' defects.
It will rob you of your merit.
It will destroy your worth.

321. Addiction takes many forms
and everyone can find his own.
A sinner can indulge his cravings
by maligning others.
Muktananda, indulge in virtue;
only praise others.

322. A man who does not seek to inflict pain
or talk ill of the bad
reveals a pure heart.
A pure heart sees everyone as pure.

VI. Destiny and Time

Destiny and Time

323. The laws of the Master of destiny
      are strong.
      One's own wishes are futile.
      Muktananda, a man reaps the fruit
      of his own actions.

324. One husband, one wife,
      one mantra, a one-pointed mind—
      Muktananda, such loyalty is the gift
      of kind destiny,
      the reward of spiritual endeavor.

325. If you are obstructed in doing good
      it is because of your past karma.
      Muktananda, suffer it cheerfully.

326. By destiny, riches.
      By destiny, poverty.
      Destiny assumes many forms
      and always walks ahead of us.
      Muktananda, destiny is joy
      as well as sorrow.

Destiny and Time

327. Destiny brings good fortune,
destiny brings bad.
Muktananda, why envy
another's triumph?
Only destiny brings change.

328. The poverty that once was is now gone.
The riches that are now were not then.
The present is as unstable as the past.
Muktananda, achieve freedom from desire.

329. The inevitable happens in its own time.
Why such hope, why such despair?
The inevitable came and it went away.
Muktananda, why do you weep, remembering?

330. Your sorrow is your self-created karma.
Looking at others
will only increase your sorrow.
Muktananda, improve your karma.

Destiny and Time

331. That which was not, came.
That which came must go.
Muktananda, remain calm and steady
in the midst of all that comes and goes.

332. What is inevitable must happen.
You cannot prevent it.
Muktananda, recognize the inevitable.
Remain tranquil in yourself.

333. This brief life passes quickly
and in the end one dies.
Now is the time, Muktananda,
to meditate on the Self.

334. The man who sees time as God
does all his work on time.
Muktananda, time is infinitely valuable.
Time is lost only in time.
Once gone it cannot be recovered.

Destiny and Time

335. You can give everything to others
but do not give them your time.
Muktananda, see God standing between
two instants of wasted time.

336. Muktananda, time once passed
does not return.
Time is pervaded by God.
Understand the importance of time.
Offer it up in meditation on the Self.

VII. KNOWLEDGE

Student, Teacher, Knowledge

337. A student should be pure, calm, single-minded, free from attachment and aversion.

338. A student who works single-mindedly obtains all glory.

339. During the time of learning, a student should not participate in anything distracting.

340. To lead a student away from learning and towards sectarian controversies and politics is reprehensible in a leader and brings degradation to the student.

341. A student whose heart is pure and who leads a regular and ideal life becomes worthy of honor.

Student, Teacher, Knowledge

342. Receive knowledge as you receive a mantra—
with reverence and respect.

343. When you pass an examination,
the goddess of knowledge
gives great joy. When you fail,
she brings misery and agony.

344. To be immersed in learning
and to learn with devotion
is itself success.

345. When students respect teachers,
that respect brings great joy.

346. To treat students with respect
is the dharma of teachers.

347. Only when student,
teacher, and knowledge become one,
is knowledge transmitted without obstruction
and in its completeness.

KNOWLEDGE

348. Gather knowledge
with single-minded devotion.
A man with a promiscuous mind
cannot succeed in anything.

349. While knowledge is being sifted and gathered,
knowledge, the giver of knowledge,
and the seeker of knowledge
should become one.

350. Learn all skills,
the mundane as well as the spiritual.

351. Knowledge is wealth, divinity, beauty.
Know that one who lacks knowledge
is worthless.
Muktananda, find knowledge.

352. Knowledge reveals the path of peace,
grants godliness,
makes man Narayana.
Muktananda, obtain knowledge.

Receive God's Message

353. A reporter came to me and said,
"Great-souled one, give a message."
I replied, "Friend, what is the use
of spreading a message in the world
if you remain deprived
of the message of God?
If my message leads you to God,
then it will be worth hearing."

354. If a man is enlightened enough
to give a message,
that message reaches God.
From God it is returned to the universe.

355. These days everyone regards giving a message
as the best thing he can do.
Muktananda, who will listen to the message
of one who has not received the message?

KNOWLEDGE

356. Muktananda, why make men weak
      by transmitting feeble messages to them,
      when you yourself have not received the message
      of the supreme God and the Guru?

357. When a man has not received
      the supreme message of God,
      what purpose is served
      by the human message
      that he sends out into the world?

358. Muktananda, to give a message
      when you have not received it from God
      is simply play-acting.

359. O Reformer! Message-giver!
      Reform your heart and receive God's message.

360. Muktananda, immerse yourself
      in Nityananda's ocean;
      become the water
      of the ocean of Nityananda.
      Only then will your messages become perfect.

Receive God's Message

361. When you receive enlightenment from God,
    a message from Him to impart messages,
    then, Muktananda,
    you will be worthy of giving a message.

362. What charity can a poor man give?
    If he lacks virtue,
    can a man give a discourse on virtue?
    If you have not received the message,
    Muktananda, what message will you give?

363. First receive the message,
    then let it take root.
    After that, inspiration will spring forth,
    and your message will reach the world
    of its own accord.

364. The message of God
    is fully revealed, ever illumined.
    Try to listen to it.

*K*NOWLEDGE

365. Every day the sun rises in the morning
and sets in the evening.
Every day, day by day, one day is lost.
In this way, life comes to an end.
Listen to the message revealed by the sun.

366. Through thousands of years of history
great and glorious kings and emperors
vanished while they were still being honored.
We, too, have seen many pass by.
We, too, will soon depart.
We must prepare food and funds
for the journey.
We should receive the message of mortality
from those who have departed.

367. The kingdoms of kings,
the wealth of the wealthy,
the strength of the strong,
all pass like dreams in time.
Muktananda, is it not a message from the Divine
that all life perishes?

Receive God's Message

368. Muktananda, see party, faction,
country, prosperity,
as wind-blown clouds wandering in the sky.
In these look for the message
that will take you beyond desire
and bring you to the inner Self.

369. Muktananda, titles like Bharat-ratna
and Padmabhushan,
the honor and praise received in daily life,
are nothing more than plastic fruits and flowers,
when the divine message is not present.

370. Muktananda, make your life exemplary.
Live in accordance with the divine message.
Then you will not be harassed
by giving message after message.

Inner Knowledge, Outer Knowledge

371. There is everything in inner understanding.
Acquire it.
Brother Muktananda,
if you have understanding you can be happy
even in the midst of suffering.

372. Understanding is eye,
understanding is light.
Without it a man is worthless.
Muktananda, acquire inner understanding.
There is nothing greater.

373. Obtain inner knowledge.
It is infinitely precious.
Muktananda, meditation culminates
in knowledge.

374. Glibness is not knowledge.
Discourses may flow from an empty mind.
Muktananda, true knowledge
is the direct inspiration
of the Self.

*K*NOWLEDGE

375. You can find the highest bliss,
not by talking Vedanta,
but by following its directions.

376. The world is much in need
of those who believe the Vedantic truth
and live in accordance with it.
But if you have not practiced that truth,
can you speak about it?

377. The man who has seen Rama in his own heart
sees Him in everyone's heart.
But if you have not seen Him within,
will you find any happiness
in talking about Him to other people?

378. The heart itself is Vaikuntha,
Bhuloka, Goloka, and Kailas.
If you have not seen Him in the heart,
why do you babble about Vaikuntha?

Inner Knowledge, Outer Knowledge

379. The inspiration of the heart
surpasses all learning.
Muktananda, find inspiration
through Nityananda's grace.

380. Through the verses of true poets,
in the mantras of the Upanishads,
speaks the ecstasy of the Self.
Inner knowledge is greater
than the knowledge that comes from books.

381. There are millions of poets
but the divinely inspired one is rare.
An ordinary poet is without true foundation.
Muktananda, God's poet is the poet of the Self.

382. Muktananda,
what is the use of human poetry?
It is like horns on a hare
or a mirage in the desert.

KNOWLEDGE

383. A poet who speaks without understanding,
describes without seeing,
repeats without hearing—
Muktananda, that poet without experience
is barren.

384. The poet whose speech is inspired by the Guru,
whose acts are inspired by Hari,
whose poetry illumines by God's light—
what that great poet says, God said.

385. Muktananda, how far can learning take you
if you are without the grace of the inner Self?

386. Muktananda, your knowledge is from books,
your learning without experience.
How can you transmit the Guru's knowledge?

Inner Knowledge, Outer Knowledge

387. He has read the four Vedas,
mastered the arts.
In the intricacies of Sanskrit grammar
there is no one better.
His intellect is penetrating
and above all he is a great bhakta.
But, Muktananda,
without inner knowledge
he is a blind man.

388. He can speak like Brihaspati.
His nadis are purified.
He is as beautiful as Shukamuni.
He has the strength of Bhima.
He organizes and manages better than anyone.
Muktananda, in spite of this,
if he is without inner knowledge,
he is as if he were not.

389. You have studied the scriptures.
You have acquired all arts
and received degrees.
But, Muktananda,
because your inner Shakti
is not awake,
you have no peace.

KNOWLEDGE

390. God's grace is full of wonder.
It constantly pours forth.
Obsession with scriptural knowledge
is ignorance.
Muktananda,
the awakening caused by the Guru
is all that matters.

391. Muktananda,
your thoughts are your world.
Let Nityananda live in your thoughts.

392. Nityananda, the supremely adored,
lives in all men.
Muktananda, you suffer needlessly
because you lack this knowledge.

393. Do not see injustice in God's justice.
Do not look for bad logic in right reasoning.
Muktananda,
cast off the turban of learning.
Be drunk with ecstasy.

Inner Knowledge, Outer Knowledge

394. When reading the *Gita*,
become Krishna;
when listening to it,
become Arjuna.
When reciting the *Yoga Vasishtha*,
become Vasishtha;
when listening to it,
become Rama.
You will attain the immortal elixir at once.

395. To be without knowledge is misery.
Muktananda, receive the Guru's knowledge.
It creates Kailas on earth.

396. By day and by night
the same air gives life
to all beings.
The same earth gives shelter
to both renunciant and sensualist.
Similarly, perfect knowledge leads
the householder, the sadhu, and the sannyasi
to Nityananda.

KNOWLEDGE

397. For the ignorant
the world is full of sorrow.
For the empty-hearted it is empty.
But for lovers of the Guru
it is full of promise.
When the Guru's knowledge arises
from within, you see the play of the Self
everywhere.

VIII. Mind, Meditation, Japa

Mind

398. A mind detached and desireless,
a stillness free of all craving,
absolute contentment in the heart—
That, Muktananda, is Satchidananda,
the supreme Being.

399. Man's mind
is his own heaven or hell.
Muktananda,
don't perform the yajna of hell
in your mind.

400. Without the grace of the mind
even in heaven you will be without peace.
Muktananda, obtain that grace.
Then you can be called truly human.

401. There is no devotion without thought,
no Shakti without devotion.
If a man is without Shakti,
where will he find peace?

Mind

402. Peace of mind is lasting peace.
Peace of mind is truly life.
What is a man without peace of mind?

403. Unless the mind is dispassionate
how can it be tranquil?
Without control of the mind and senses
how can there be sadhana?
Unless the sense of 'I' is destroyed
how can there be Self-realization?

404. Muktananda, God revels in your heart,
yet your mind is engrossed elsewhere.
It contemplates faults.
What a great wonder!

405. Chiti fills the mind.
Muktananda, this is your good fortune.
Why then do you contemplate sin?

Mind, Meditation, Japa

406. The wealth of the mind,
the delight of the mind,
the good of the mind,
is in contemplation of Chiti.
Muktananda, give up contemplating
the faults of others.

407. Muktananda,
you have obtained the rare human form.
Now you must leave your obsession with evil.
Only then will your life be fulfilled.
Only then will you be blessed.

408. Dissolve the mind.
You will become Mahadeva.
While the mind remains,
you will stay in bondage.

409. God is ever present.
Look within the heart.
Because the mind is impure,
you think He is not there.

Mind

410. O man, you are not a bound creature.
You are the life-giving God.
When you receive the gift of Sri Guru's grace,
you will understand this.

411. The mind weeps in a bad dream,
not knowing it is only dreaming.
The mind also weeps without cause
in the waking state—
because it lacks knowledge.

412. In the mind, Ganga and Kashi.
In the mind, worship and meditation.
In the mind, knowledge.
In the mind, Rama and Shiva.
Muktananda, if not in the mind,
nowhere else.

413. Worship the mind.
Meditate on the mind.
Revere the mind.
The mind is everything.
If there is no worship,
meditation, reverence in the mind,
where else will you find them?

414. Keep your mind cheerful at all times;
it will help you to achieve true calm.
If the mind is not steady,
what do you have?

415. One who is master of his mind
becomes great and glorious,
and gains fame and honor in the world.
The master of the mind
is the one whose mind is steady.

416. In this world a beggar,
if he has a steady mind,
is in fact better than an emperor.

417. By the mind, the man.
Don't think that the mind is unimportant.
The mind is indeed heaven or hell.

418. If a man does not have a steady mind,
what else is he but a beggar—
even if he is very rich
and rules over the whole world?

Mind

419. Can an unstable mind sleep happily?
Can it live with love?
What peace will it find?
Tell me, Muktananda.

420. The world is heaven
for one whose mind is pure and noble,
in spite of all hardships.

421. Muktananda, what's the use
of being the head of the richest monastery
if the mind is not pure,
if the intellect is not steady,
and if the reason lacks discrimination?

422. Muktananda, your own mind
is the root of high and low,
honor and insult,
joy and sorrow.

423. God is full of bliss.
Brother, why do you weep?
He appears to be far
because your mind is not pure.

424. You remain far from peace
because you make your mind filthy.
Make your mind clean and pure.
You will find both peace and happiness.

425. First purify the body,
then control the senses,
then perform good deeds.
Purify prana-apana.
Recite ajapa-japa.
Cleanse the heart and speech
by reciting the *Gita* and the *Sahasranama*.
In this way you will win the grace of the mind.

Path of Meditation

426. Meditate on your Self.
The sadhana of meditation
is perfect sadhana.
Parashiva is within you.
He is yours.

427. In the center of the head,
in the center of the sahasrara,
Parashiva and Shakti revel joyfully.
Muktananda, reach them
by the path of meditation.

428. I sought sweetness in external beauty
and in the end found none.
Muktananda, joy is within.
Meditate.

Mind, Meditation, Japa

429. Meditate.
Do not let your mind be tempted,
for the world is mutable
and changes from moment to moment.

430. Muktananda, the mind,
in its ever-deepening inward plunge,
disdains the allurements of the world.

431. Relinquish appearances,
for they are illusion.
Relinquish the turmoil of the world,
for it is perishable.
Find rapture in the awareness
of the vibrating Consciousness,
the Consciousness that pervades
everything.

Path of Meditation

432. When the senses
are touched by the Guru's grace
they forget their love of external things
and steadily turn inward.
The inner region of the heart
is God's region.
Now, this very moment,
meditate on the inner Being.

433. You get some peace through sleep.
You know this, Muktananda.
Why then question the perfect peace
that comes through meditation?

434. Pleasure and pain, gain and loss,
are experienced only
in a certain state of mind.
Muktananda, in meditation on the Self
there is only the one perfect bliss.

435. The concerns of waking
are irrelevant in sleep.
What is real in dreams
is unreal in waking.
Only peace can enter turiya.

Mind, Meditation, Japa

436. Muktananda, meditate for supreme peace.
Do not worry about meditation.
Whatever your condition, meditate.

437. As you close your eyes and sleep at night,
so, Muktananda,
wherever you are, however you are,
forget your mind
and meditate on your Self.

438. Meditation depends
on the inclination to meditate
and on nothing else.
Muktananda, meditate with love.

439. As a bird soars, sees his prey and swoops,
as an arrow flies from the bow,
so a yogi plunges into the Self
and sees the divine light.

Path of Meditation

440. Let all your thoughts,
 good and bad,
 come and go as they will.
 Rid yourself of vain imaginings.
 Receive inspiration from within.
 Meditation will then come of itself.

441. You do not control your mind.
 It roams with the roaming senses.
 Muktananda, turn within.
 Focus on the inner light.
 Be in the transcendental state of bliss.

442. Knowing all the movements of the mind
 to be movements of Chiti,
 meditate on the One-in-all everywhere.
 Muktananda, when Chiti Herself is the mind,
 what difference does it make
 if you are meditating or not?

443.	You are your own mantra, *So'ham*.
	You are the technique of your own meditation.
	When you are meditation,
	the object of your meditation
	and the meditator,
	you are your own Guru.

444.	The Master hidden in your inner cave
	pervades all forms.
	Why don't you see Him
	through the natural yajna of meditation?

445.	The universe expands from the blissful Lord.
	The universe is the Master who pervades it.
	Muktananda, explore the inner land
	in meditation.
	There is so much ambrosia!

Fruits of Meditation

446. Through meditation
the object of meditation is easily attained.
Muktananda,
immerse your mind in meditation.

447. Meditation gives the desired fruit.
It stabilizes the mind
and is the vehicle that carries you
to the city of liberation.
Become immersed in meditation.

448. In meditation
the prana becomes steady.
The body is freed from disease and is purified.
Therefore, worship meditation.

449. By meditation
you are released from addictions.
It cleanses the sense of taste.
It sharpens the intellect.
Therefore,
worship meditation.

450. Meditation is the home of health.
It strengthens the body.
Through meditation you sleep joyful sleep.
Truly, it is heaven.

451. By meditation posture is mastered.
Inspiration and prosperity are attained.
The senses are fulfilled.
Deficiencies are made good.

452. Meditation has the power
to make possible the impossible,
to make attainable the unattainable.

453. Muktananda,
a mind without meditation,
a mind that lacks one-pointedness,
a life without knowledge—
these are as dry as an oasis in a mirage.

Fruits of Meditation

454. Full knowledge, supreme bliss, perfection—
all arise through meditation.
Muktananda,
only by meditation
does the knowledge gained from the scriptures
become a living experience.

455. Paise add up to thousands of rupees.
Trees, which grow every day,
one day produce blossoms and fruit.
Drops add up to an ocean.
Meditate every day,
and you will create an ocean of peace.

456. In meditation the 'I' is lost.
The sense of 'I' is merged
in pure, eternally blissful Consciousness—
Only Shiva, the supreme Being, remains.
Are you not that Shiva?
Give up the delusion
"I am made of flesh."

Mind, Meditation, Japa

457. By meditation
divinity is attained
and birth and death end.
By meditation
the Self is realized.
Meditation
is truly Nityananda.

458. In meditation the mind delights,
the heart rejoices.
Compared to the one who meditates
even Indra is a beggar.

459. The mantra of peace is meditation.
Peace is the fruit of meditation.
Meditation is the deity of peace.
O man, attain peace.

460. What is life without peace?
What happiness comes without peace?
Peace comes by meditation.
O Muktananda,
attain meditation.

Meditation on Your Self

461. Meditation on your Self
is meditation on Rama.
Worship of your Self
is worship of God.
Bowing to your Self
is bowing to the Guru's feet.
Contemplation of your Self
is repetition of the mahamantra.
Muktananda, see your Self.
You are glorious.

462. Meditation on your Self
is bathing in the Ganges.
Meditation on your Self
is all worship.
Meditation on your Self
is all merit.
Muktananda, meditate on your Self.

463. Meditation on your Self
is yoga.
Meditation on your Self
is bathing in holy waters.
Meditation on your Self is your duty.
Muktananda, meditate on your Self.

464. Meditation on your Self
is all the fire rituals.
Meditation on your Self
is eternal dharma.
Meditation on your Self
is perfect worship.
Muktananda, lose yourself in *So'ham*.

465. Meditation on your Self
is meditation on Rama.
Meditation on your Self
is meditation on Krishna.
Meditation on your Self
is worship of Shiva.
Meditation on your Self
is mahayajna.
Muktananda, leave other forms.
Meditate on your Self.

Meditation on Your Self

466. Lose yourself in meditation on your Self.
Losing yourself you will find your Self in all.
Muktananda, to lose yourself
is to find your Self.

467. The red aura is the size of the body
and represents its gross form.
You will see it
as you see an object in the world.
Meditate on your Self
and you will see it clearly.
Muktananda,
why speak without direct experience?

468. The white flame is the size of your thumb
and stands for the subtle body of the soul.
Meditating daily,
you will see it in the center of sleep.
When you do not know your own inner body
what's the good of knowing anything else?

469. The causal body is black-complexioned.
It is the size of a fingertip and very beautiful.
See it, Muktananda, in deep meditation,
the prime cause of birth and death.
Deeper still you will see your true form.

470. In the center of the heart-space —
a cave no larger than your thumb —
bliss trickles
from the sky-blue light.
Muktananda,
lose yourself in meditation.
Drink that bliss.

471. The blue light is the size of a sesame seed.
It is the source of all bodies.
It is the house of your soul.

472. Meditate with love, Muktananda.
You will find the blue light.
By attaining this you can attain everything.

Meditation on Your Self

473. The light of the heart's Lord blazes brightly.
Muktananda, enter the heart.
See the sky-blue river of bliss.

474. When your mind is immersed in meditation
you will see the blue firmament.
The light of Consciousness
forever glows and sparkles there.

By Japa, Life

475. If your meditation is full of japa,
if your mind is not restless,
if you contemplate with love,
how far can Kailas be?

476. By japa, meditation.
By japa, yoga.
By japa, love.
By japa, direct knowledge.
Muktananda, do ajapa-japa.
Parashiva is in you.

477. While getting up, Name.
While sitting, Name.
While sleeping, Name.
While working, *Rama* and *Rama* alone.
With this japa, who needs tapasya?

By Japa, Life

478. Become the owner
of the name of Rama or Keshava
by becoming one with it.

479. *Om Namah Shivaya* is the redeeming
mahamantra.
Through this mantra
you cross the world of change
without pain.

480. Continuously repeat the mahamantra,
Om Namah Shivaya.
It has been sung by sages,
seers, renunciants, and Siddhas.
In Kaliyuga, the five-syllable mantra
is supremely holy.

481. The five-syllable mantra
has infinite power.
It comes from Parashiva.
Always do this japa.

482. The high and the low,
the ignorant and the learned,
the holy and the fallen,
men and women,
all have been graced
by the five-syllable mantra.
It is the mother and source
of the seventy million mantras.

483. The five-syllable mantra
encompasses all deities, all sacred places.
The universe arises and subsides in it.
Muktananda, always do japa of it.

484. Goddess Chiti becomes pleased
when you repeat your revered mantra
with love.
Mantra is one of Her forms.

485. While bathing, while eating,
while coming and going,
continuously repeat *Om Namah Shivaya*
in prana-apana.
You will be redeemed at once.

By Japa, Life

486. Whatever your circumstances,
whatever your occupation,
continuously repeat the mantra
with a pure mind.
Muktananda, you will obtain
lasting peace.

487. Sri Guru, mantra,
mantra-deity and you—
all are one.
Repeat the mantra with this awareness.

488. Shiva is neither Shaivite
nor Vaishnava, nor Buddhist.
He is your Self.
Shiva is neither Hindu
nor Moslem, nor Christian.
He is the Self of all.
Shiva is inner bliss.
Shiva is boundless love.
Always do japa of the name of Shiva.

Mind, Meditation, Japa

Natural Japa

489. It is in terms of the body alone
that you are male or female.
Don't do the japa
"I am the body."
Through attachment to the body
man becomes stupid.
He cannot become immersed
in the bliss of the Self
that comes from the japa of *So'ham*.

490. You are different from the body.
You are the highest Shiva,
whose nature is bliss.
Always repeat *Shivo'ham*.
Whatever mantra one repeats,
that is what one becomes.
Therefore, worship Shiva.
Don't always worship the body.

Natural Japa

491. Always do japa.
It is a yajna that grants abundant fruit.
Repeat the mahamantra.
Let it fill your life.
"By japa, realization."
Thus spoke Mahadeva.
Have faith in these words.
"Japa is our greatest riddhi."
So speaks the Uplifter of the mountain,
the King of mountains.

492. Japa is yoga,
and through it man receives
the fruit he desires.

493. Let everyone do japa.
It is the form of Rama
and yields copious fruit.
So'ham is the inner ajapa-japa.
Repeat it constantly
and you will become free from sin.

494. Do ajapa-japa
and you will receive Nityananda's grace.

Mind, Meditation, Japa

495. Do japa within, in the heart, in solitude.
Do it with the loyalty
that a true wife gives her husband.
Through constant japa,
yogis unite with Brahman.
Do japa ceaselessly
and you will see your own nature within.
By repeating *So'ham-Hamsa*,
you will become Shiva.

496. Understand that it is God's inspiration
which gives spontaneous japa.
Bhagawan Nityananda is always present
in sahaja-japa.
By this natural japa
you will reach the city of liberation,
the city full of joy.
You will attain the state
that is deathless and everlasting.

Natural Japa

497. Sahaja-japa never stops.
Understanding this,
practice sahaja-japa.
With the sound *sah*,
the outgoing breath...
with the sound *ham*,
the incoming breath...
Reverse it.
With *sah* do inner japa,
with *ham* outer japa.
So'ham is the ajapa-japa.
If you repeat it without ceasing,
you are rid of virtue and sin.

498. O man, have you forgotten
to perceive that place
in which the universe is merged,
where the illusion of many
is totally dissolved?
That is non-dual, pure, supreme bliss.
It is indeed your own true name and form.
Why don't you do japa of That?

499. As you have totally succeeded
in becoming mortal,
miserable, and small
by identifying yourself as the body,
as "I, I,"
why will you not succeed
in becoming ageless, deathless,
happy, and tranquil
by identifying yourself with *So'ham, So'ham*?

500. Is there a more poisonous vine than the tongue
that abandons the name of Rama,
gives up truth, ceases japa,
and speaks only lies and inanities?

501. The inner mantra is the mahamantra.
Understand the inner mantra
and do that japa.

502. Ajapa-japa continues day and night.
So'ham, So'ham.
Hear this inner japa every moment.
Muktananda, the ajapa is pure.

Natural Japa

503. With every inhalation and exhalation
So'ham repeats itself.
Muktananda, why do your eyes wander?
Just watch the movement of prana-apana.

504. Listen to the divine chant of *So'ham*.
The breath goes in *So* and comes out *ham*.
Muktananda, the inner chant of *So'ham*
is the pure chant
in the space of Consciousness.

505. Because I lacked Self-knowledge
I thought I was incomplete.
When *So'ham* arose, I saw,
"I am perfect within myself."

506. The Self is the true God.
Have no doubt, no anxiety.
Your own Self is perfect in itself.
Muktananda, always repeat *So'ham*.

507. *Om* becomes active
and assumes a two-fold form.
Om is *So'ham*.
By *So'ham*, *Om* is reached.

508. *Om*, universe.
Om, bhakta.
Om, gods and goddesses.
The world issues from *Om*.
Muktananda, you are *Om*.

509. *Om*, man.
Om, woman.
Om, cosmos and the soul of the cosmos.
The cosmos, made of *Om*, is also *Om*.
Muktananda, *Om* is Nityananda.

510. *Om* is Brahman in the form of one syllable.
This is what the scriptures say.
Om is all.
Om is Truth.
Om is Self.
Muktananda, Nityananda, and Ganeshpuri
are *Om*.

Natural Japa

511. *Om* vibrates in freedom.
      It is the Word
      in the space of Parabrahman.
      It vibrates in the space of your heart.
      Muktananda, listen in meditation.
      Your heart will be glad.

512. The mahamantra resounds endlessly
      in the inner space.
      It speaks without tongue.
      As you hear it the immortal elixir
      wells up.
      Muktananda, hear it in meditation
      in the space of the heart.
      Then you will dance
      in rapture and intoxication.

513. There is eternal ajapa-japa
      in the heart-space.
      Drink the sap of the ajapa-nada.
      It is very sweet.
      After this, man does not die
      nor is he reborn to suffer.

514. All the world's sweetness
is in the nectar of inner nada.
In the outside world
there is only its shadow.
Muktananda, go to the source.

515. The elixir of nada
is the great elixir.
The elixir of nada
is the elixir of immortality.
As I drank this in meditation
death ceased to exist.
Muktananda is alive.

IX. Guru

Marks of a True Guru

516. Depending on nothing but himself,
expecting nothing,
completely independent and unattached—
Muktananda,
these are the marks of Sri Guru.

517. A Guru should only be a Guru.
If a Guru is not perfect,
his disciple is not perfect either.

518. The one who saw himself fully in Brahman,
and Brahman fully in himself,
and who worshiped without differentiation—
Muktananda,
he is Guru Nityananda.

Marks of a True Guru

519. Muktananda,
the Guru who frees disciples
of discipleship,
who transforms their world
into a haven of the spirit,
who bestows his own state upon them,
is deserving of supreme adoration.

520. If the land has never been sown,
what will grow there?
If the seed-bestowing Guru
is not there himself,
how will knowledge arise?

521. Living far from loss and gain;
living by principles and faith,
with a mind that sees all as equal;
being just and fair to everyone
and always perfectly unattached—
these are the characteristics of Sri Guru.

Guru

522. Muktananda,
that Guru is worthy of reverence
for whom equality is a natural state,
who despises separateness,
and who is the enemy of duality,
the friend of unity.

523. He has no trace of bondage.
He changes the bondage of others
into divinity.
His vision is one.
Such is the Guru.

524. He regards the animate
and the inanimate as himself.
He sees all men as his children,
and imparts right teaching to them
as the householder guides equally
all children in his house.
Such a Guru,
Muktananda,
is the image of God.

Marks of a True Guru

525.   He who transmits his Shakti to the disciple
and makes him aware of Brahman,
and who unifies the individual soul,
the universe, and Brahman,
is Sri Gurudeva.

526.   He who awakens the Shakti
that pierces the six chakras,
who activates that Shakti
in a disciple's entire life —
Muktananda,
worship that Guru.

527.   A perfect knower of Brahman,
a master of yoga,
fully established in the inner Self —
Muktananda,
know that Guru to be perfect.

Guru

528. In his company,
sadhana succeeds easily.
Even the hardest task
becomes simple and natural.
Just by living with him
there is inner awakening
and one becomes absorbed in the Self.
Muktananda,
that is Guru Nityananda;
always live with him.

529. Muktananda,
through the inner awakening
bestowed by the Guru
you will not just become a jivanmukta;
from an ordinary person
you will become the Supreme Person.

530. Muktananda,
the man who receives
the full blessing of Sri Guru
is blessed by everyone.

Marks of a False Guru

531. If he has assumed the role of Guru
while still not perfect,
keep away from him.

532. If he is everyone's Guru
but was no one's disciple,
he is nothing but a pestilence.

533. If he claims he is realized
but teaches the yoga of drugs, alcohol, and sex,
is he a Guru or a messenger from hell?

534. If he cannot sleep at night
because his disciples might leave him
in the morning,
if he lets the disciples do what they like
and does not believe in discipline,
he bears all the marks of a Guru
who is not a Guru.

Guru

535. "To live with a Guru and stay in bondage"
 ... is that possible?

536. If he changes the color of your clothes
 without changing the color of your heart,
 is he a Guru or a dyer?

537. Muktananda, isn't a beast better
 than one who sits on the seat of the Guru,
 not for the disciples' good,
 but for his own ambition and glory?

538. You have learned so much to instruct others,
 nothing for your own understanding.
 The respected pandit
 and the respected maulavi are the same—
 they only teach others,
 but don't learn themselves.

539. If you have not been given any experience
 of the inner Self
 and are lost in clever terms
 and new techniques,
 you can be sure you are with a false guru.

Marks of a False Guru

540.   If he cannot transmit the Shakti,
       if Kundalini is not awakened in his company,
       he is a pretender, not a Guru.

541.   If he robs you of your money
       but not of your misery,
       isn't he the greatest swindler of all?

542.   He can cure a running nose
       but not self-seeking;
       he can produce sacred ash and tennis balls
       but not inner bliss;
       he can give words but not love—
       Muktananda, such a one is God's curse.

Guru's Grace

543. Whether you are a renunciant or a yogi,
a bhakta or a jnani,
the essential thing is Guru's grace.

544. On the path of spirituality and peace
the Guru is foremost.
Without him there are only barren seeds.

545. In his journey through life
a man meets many people who appeal to him
and become his friends.
Some friendships are short, others long.
But only the Sadguru
is a true and lasting friend,
only he truly deserves this name.

546. A man absorbed in meditation
is dedicated to the inner world.
He does not dirty himself
in the external world.
Muktananda, always bathe in the Ganges
of the Guru's love.

Guru's Grace

547. Inner bliss begins to throb
only when the Guru
gives his full blessing.
It is not commonplace.
Inner bliss belongs to the house of God.
Why do you consider it your creation,
Muktananda?

548. When the mind stops
without concentration,
when prana stops
without forced kumbhaka,
when the eyes are still
though not fixed on an object,
you know the mudra of Guru's grace.

549. The mudra of Guru's grace is mahamudra.
It has countless names:
Khechari, Shambhavi, Parashiva-shakti-mudra.
Muktananda, obtain it by Sri Guru's blessing.

Guru's Grace

550. O seeker,
receive the mudra of Sri Guru's grace.
Through this there is peace.
See it in everyone with the Guru's eye.

551. Guru's grace, divine grace.
Attainment of Guru,
attainment of everything.
Gurumudra, mahamudra.
Muktananda, only a rare fortunate one
receives that mudra.

552. I speak the truth.
Within you there is peace that is free,
perfect, and wonderfully sweet.
Muktananda, without Guru's grace
no one has yet attained it.

553. God and Guru give everything
but man does not know how to take.
Muktananda, what is the use of taking
just a little?

Guru

554.   Become worthy of Sri Guru's grace
and you will easily swim across
the ocean of worldliness.
The world is without nectar.
What happiness will you gain without grace?

555.   How can a foolish man
ever attain the immortal state
of supreme bliss without grace?
By Nityananda's grace
a man swims across samsara with ease.

556.   By the grace of God,
man becomes God.
Separateness vanishes.
By the grace of Shiva,
man becomes Shiva.
He swims across samsara.
By the grace of knowledge,
a fool becomes wise.
Muktananda,
by the grace of Sri Guru,
a man becomes perfect,
and attains supreme bliss.

Guru's Grace

557. By grace, Gopi Chand was freed
from attachment to the senses
and became immortal;
by grace, Eklavya mastered
the art of archery;
by the gift of Sri Guru's grace,
you will sleep joyful sleep.

558. Without Guru's grace,
life is arid and depressing.
Man is inextricably caught in samsara,
the relentless disease of mutability
and becoming,
and suffers greatly.
By the Guru's grace,
Muktananda transcended death.

559. Grace makes man God,
the jiva Brahman, a mortal immortal.
Is life not death without it?

560. By Guru's grace, Kundalini's grace;
by Her grace, the unfolding of your life;
and from that unfolding,
the attainment of supreme bliss.

GURU

561. Without Sri Guru's compassion,
      man is an insect in hell.
      He sinks in the pit of becoming.
      Without the Guru's compassion,
      life is eternal weeping.
      Muktananda, when you lacked Sri Guru's grace,
      what peace did you find?

562. Gurudev bestowed his grace
      and Kundalini awoke.
      Muktananda's star rose.
      Fear and pettiness fled.

563. By the radiance of the inner Shakti
      I attained full inner purity.
      I saw the conscious light of Chiti
      shimmering.
      I received the gift of Guru's grace
      in this very body.

Guru's Grace

564. Sri Guru's grace is the ferry.
It takes you across the ocean of samsara.
It carries you to the center
of the city of liberation.
It takes you to the true state of Nityananda.
Muktananda, gain Sri Guru's grace.

565. The mantra that the Guru gives you in secret
must be repeated resolutely and in secret.
A seed sown in the earth
grows in time into a vast tree
bearing blossoms and fruit.
In exactly the same way,
the grace of the Guru
holds all powers and realizations.

566. The Guru is neither God nor individual.
He is just the Guru,
who destroys darkness and gives light.

567. Darkness is not obliterated without the sun,
nor cold without heat, nor hunger without food.
In the same way,
without knowledge imparted by the Guru,
ignorance is not destroyed.

Guru

568. Obtain the grace of Hari-Guru.
You will find immortality.
Grace fills the heart with joy.
Grace takes you to the realm
of divine knowledge.
As grace is the nature of God,
you experience God in it.
Because he obtained Guru Nityananda's grace,
Muktananda became immortal.

569. Without the gift of grace,
you will not develop faith
in the mahaprasad,
in Govinda,
in the divine Name,
in supreme Brahman, in Shiva,
and in the purity of a Vaishnava.
When God becomes pleased,
He grants His own nature.
Therefore obtain Nityananda's grace,
and happiness and peace will be given to you.

570. Prasad is filled with God.
See Him in it.
When you receive mahaprasad,
mantraprasad, Guruprasad,
your good fortune begins.
Without Guru's grace,
you cannot cross samsara.
Attain Nityananda's prasad
and become liberated while still in this body.

571. Yajnaprasad, Guruprasad
and mantraprasad are great.
God's prasad and Guruprasad
bear abundant fruit.
When grace bears fruit,
complete transformation occurs.
By Nityananda's blessing,
Muktananda effortlessly attained yoga.

572. Until you are established in inner bliss,
seek grace.
When you live contented in your Self,
you have received grace fully.
Don't become miserable by forgetting your Self
and looking for satisfaction outside.
Go within.
You will receive Nityananda's blessing.

Guru

573. Muktananda, if by Sri Guru's blessing
you are established in the transcendental state,
you will find peace on thorns—
peace even in the hangman's noose.

574. Guru's grace intoxicates the mind
with happiness and bliss,
and in the end grants the divine state
of absolute aloneness.

575. Who knows
where mental conflicts may lead one,
the torments they may compel one to suffer?
Life is really very difficult
without Sri Guru's grace.

576. There is no friend equal to the Guru,
who makes everyone equal to himself.
There is no enemy equal to the Guru,
who destroys the state of separateness.
There is no giver equal to the Guru,
who gives the state of Brahman in a moment.
Muktananda, if you want to do anything,
serve the Guru.

Guru's Grace

577. Make friends with him
who lifts you up to his own height,
who releases you
from the snare of name and form,
and makes you as free as himself.

578. As fire
transforms everything it touches
into fire,
and as earth
turns everything placed within it
into earth,
so Muktananda,
keep company with him
who will merge you in himself.

God, Guru, and Self

579. Desire is the seed of samsara.
Muktananda, if you must desire,
desire Nityananda.

580. The world is constantly changing.
It is a phenomenon of the mind.
Muktananda, let your mind be filled
with Nityananda.

581. Muktananda, devotion to the Guru
is the wish-fulfilling vine.
Day and night, meditate on Nityananda.

582. When you love the Guru
as you love the world,
the world is filled with Nityananda.

God, Guru, and Self

583. Shiva is better than jiva,
Narayana is better than nara,
Self is better than ego.
Muktananda, in this life,
Nityananda is better than you.

584. Seek your Self.
Worship your Self.
Kneel to your Self.
Muktananda, Nityananda fills you.

585. He who lives in prana and activates prana,
whose vehicle is prana,
who is the prana of prana,
who is detached—
Muktananda,
He is the God of the universe.

586. He who lives in fire and makes it burn,
whose throne is fire,
who is the fire of fire—
Muktananda, that is your inner Self.

Guru

587. He who lives in the mind
 and makes the mind move,
 whose chariot is the mind,
 who is the seer of the mind,
 who is beyond the mind—
 That is Satchidananda, Guru Nityananda.

588. He who lives in the eyes
 and through them sees form,
 whose seat is the eyes,
 who is the eye of all,
 who is the great light—
 Muktananda, that is the conscious Self.

589. He who sees without eyes,
 hears without ears,
 speaks without tongue—
 Muktananda, go beyond the senses
 and see Him.

590. He who sees form through the eyes,
 who smells perfume through the nose,
 hears through the ears
 and repeats "I, I" until He knows Himself—
 Muktananda, That is the inner Narayana.

God, Guru, and Self

591. He who becomes a Guru
and transmits knowledge,
who becomes a disciple
and receives knowledge,
who becomes a mother
and nurtures and nourishes,
who becomes a father
and protects —
Muktananda, He is the same in all.

592. He is not the one who is thought
by the mind.
He is the One who makes the mind think.
He is the not-mind behind the mind.
Muktananda, know Him to be your Self.

593. The Guru is the life and wealth
of the inner Self.
He is the greatest possession.

594. There is no difference
between Guru and God.
Only God manifests Himself
in the form of the Guru.

Guru

595. When the Sadguru is satisfied
all deities give their blessings.
When the Sadguru is pleased
all mantras yield their fruit.
Worship the Guru's Self.
Have faith that it is your own Self.

596. There is one in many.
There are many in one.
Muktananda, merge the many into yourself
and yourself into Sri Guru Nityananda.

597. Faith in Guru is faith in God.
Guru's feet are God's feet.
Remembrance of Guru
is worship of Self.
Worship of Nityananda
is worship of the cosmos.

598. Muktananda, meditation on Sri Guru,
worship of Sri Guru,
remembrance of Sri Guru,
contemplation of Sri Guru,
brings the state of Nityananda.

599. Worship of Sri Guru is worship of Self.
Worship of Sri Guru is worship of Krishna.
Worship of Sri Guru is worship of the cosmos.
Muktananda, what else is there?
What else but the Guru?

X. DISCIPLE

Worthiness

600. Discipleship is the key to yoga.
It is the sadhana of knowledge
and the perfect path to liberation.
Muktananda,
become a perfect disciple.

601. All sadhanas are fulfilled in discipleship.
The true disciple gets the fruit of all austerities.
God becomes his support.
Muktananda,
become a perfect disciple.

602. Above all,
a disciple should be worthy.
Realization will come sooner or later,
according to his worth.

603. If a disciple does not become a perfect disciple,
he does not receive perfect grace.

Worthiness

604. Laziness, carelessness, inertia,
and absence of the will to serve
are not the characteristics of a disciple,
Muktananda, but of someone
who does not deserve to be a disciple.

605. In ancient times
the great seers kept their disciples
for twelve years
and exercised complete control over them.
The result was complete realization.
Without discipline,
can attainment be lasting?
A man easily falls.

606. If a disciple does not obey Sri Guru's command,
if a Shaiva is without ritual,
if a man is without character,
if a woman is without discipline—
then Muktananda,
they are not worth anything.

Disciple

607. A pure, one-pointed mind,
a simple and comfortable posture,
repetition of the Guru's name—
these are the marks of a seeker.

608. A disciple who is intelligent,
disciplined, discerning, enduring, detached,
and without identification with the body
is a worthy disciple—none other.

609. Muktananda, know that cunning and hypocrisy
in relation to the Guru
comprise the greatest discipline of corruption
and lead one off the spiritual path.

610. See him at the root of the mind
the same way you see him outside.
The inner Guru knows all your outer dealings—
and grants the fruits.

611. Muktananda,
if you want the mind to be full of peace,
let your dealings with the Guru
be completely free from cunning.

Worthiness

612. The inner Guru is omniscient.
      He keeps a perfect record
      of what you deposit and what you spend,
      of what is owed to him.
      Muktananda, live with care.

613. Jealousy, hypocrisy, malice,
      affectation, grumbling, and weeping—
      these are not the result of Guru's grace.
      Muktananda, do not bring discredit
      to the Guru's name
      by merely paying lip service to him,
      repeating, "Guru! Guru!"

614. Growing malice and hostility,
      jealousy of others' wealth,
      a zealous involvement with others' faults
      instead of remembrance of the Lord—
      Muktananda, Guru's grace does not
      make friends with these sins.

*D*ISCIPLE

615.   If peace came through hatred
and the disparagement of those
who love the Guru,
a butcher would be an ocean of peace.
The violence is the same.

616.   O revered and clever bhakta,
Sir, understand your self-deception.
You are full of hostility
and malice toward others.
You hurt them. You mourn their happiness.
Muktananda, Guru Nityananda
never taught such lessons.

617.   Recognize the Guru in everyone.
Laugh happily seeing another.
Without Nityananda's grace
it is hard to laugh only with love.

618.   Respected bhakta,
your attitude is your world.
Make your world your highest heaven.
Let the Guru's world live in your eye.

Tests of Truth

619. Only the disciple
who passes all the tests of truth
in the house of the Guru
acquires the radiance, power, discernment,
and perfection of a Siddha.

620. Don't run away because you fear hardship.
Wherever you go, hardship will be there,
standing in your path.
Muktananda, remember this.

621. Sri Rama is found in hardship.
In hardship Sri Krishna is attained.
Don't get frightened when you see hardship.
Muktananda,
it is in hardship
that the Self is realized.

Disciple

622. You love the flesh,
and because of your attachment
to the perishable body
you want to wander.
Muktananda,
can you ever convert the body
into gold?

623. Because of too many obstacles,
the impurities and defects of past lives,
you are driven to mistake
what is not worth doing for what is,
and what is worth doing for what is not.
Muktananda,
live with discrimination.

624. You are negligent,
lethargic, slow of understanding,
and your mind is immature.
Muktananda,
your mind will trip you up.
Live with firm faith in Nityananda.

Tests of Truth

625. Muktananda,
 the test at the Guru's house is hard.
 Take it with care.

626. All kinds of enemies
 will try to bring about the downfall
 of the weak, the timid, and the dependent.
 Live unswervingly
 in the sanctuary of Nityananda.

627. Kabir wept and wept
 at the sight of a grinding wheel.
 A saint said to him,
 "Kabir, don't weep.
 Look instead at the grain stuck at the hub.
 It will not be ground;
 it will remain intact."

628. Offer your mind to the Guru.
 Offer your being to the Guru.
 Entrust these to him.
 Enthrone his form in your heart.
 How far, then, is perfect bliss?

*D*ISCIPLE

629. Where else should a disciple go
who is absorbed in service to Sri Guru?
Muktananda,
your Sri Guru Nityananda,
holy and pure, embodies all sacred places.

630. The freedom of the Self is supremely good,
nectarean, worthy of honor.
Muktananda, it can only be achieved
by taking refuge in the Guru.

One-Pointedness

631. Sing the Guru's praises,
do japa of the Guru,
meditate on the Guru.
The Guru
is the highest object of adoration
in the world.

632. The Guru is the only source of knowledge
and the gallows for worldliness.
From him alone come peace and Self-fulfillment.
Muktananda, accept only Sri Guru
as your family deity.

633. Only the Guru
is the knowledge of Brahman.
In the Guru alone
is the science of yoga.
The Guru gives meditation and mantra.
Truly Muktananda,
only Gurudeva
can reveal to you
all science and knowledge.

634. If you would act,
serve Sri Guru;
if you would do japa,
repeat his name;
if you would meditate,
meditate on his form;
if you would worship,
worship his feet.
Muktananda,
worship of the Guru
contains all realizations.

635. Any deity other than the Guru,
any holy center other than his ashram,
any mantra other than *So'ham*—
Muktananda, this is promiscuity.

636. A man who says he is a bhakta
and yet holds back from the Lord, steals.
A man who gives himself to the Guru
and yet wants to go on pilgrimages
and perform rituals
also commits a small theft.

One-Pointedness

637. After one has accepted the Guru as all in all
and has offered oneself to him,
how can one take oneself back?

638. Loyalty to one's husband is great;
what is sadhana for a wife
other than serving her husband?
To whom if not to God
will a bhakta offer devotion?
Muktananda,
what can a true disciple find
in any other place
if he leaves his Guru?

639. A prostitute is nobler
than one who gives up dharma,
kingdom, husband, vows, or the Guru.

640. If a man claims to be a Gurubhakta
but does not harness body, mind, and soul
entirely to the Guru's service,
does not obey the Guru's commands implicitly,
does not think ceaselessly of the Guru,
then Muktananda,
he is only an actor.

641. Just as you may transfer all your troubles
to someone else
and become free and happy,
so if you were to give yourself
entirely to Sri Guru
you would find happiness.

642. For a true disciple,
Sri Guru's name
is the only redeeming mahamantra.
What use has the tongue
that sings the praises of Sri Guru
for any other mantra?

643. If you want to do japa,
repeat Sri Guru's name.
If you want to meditate,
meditate on his form.
If you want to perform an action,
do mental worship of Sri Guru.
Muktananda, there is nothing
like the worship of the Guru.

One-Pointedness

644. Millions become external disciples,
 but the inner disciple is rare.
 He totally surrenders
 his thoughts and feelings to the Guru—
 and attains the state of Nityananda.

645. The mark of a true disciple
 is that he gives up all desire,
 even for realization,
 and, filled with complete love for the Guru,
 joins his mind with Sri Guru Nityananda.

646. A disciple whose heart
 is full of devotion to the Guru,
 who thinks, reflects, and meditates
 only on Sri Guru,
 whose sense organs are obedient to his will—
 Muktananda, he is sacred Kashi.

647. A poor man who is full of devotion
and love for Hari-Guru
is fortunate and blessed.
A rich man who is poor in devotion
is a joyless beggar.
What is he worth?

648. You may repeat the name of Rama or Shiva,
you may learn yoga or engage in action,
but if you are not singing the Guru's praises,
you have not arrived anywhere.

649. Without boundless devotion to the Guru
a yogi is empty, a Vedantin dry,
a bhakta joyless,
and the six schools of philosophy yield nothing.
Muktananda, the real nectar
is the remembrance of Nityananda.

650. From the scriptures
and the discourses of the noble-hearted,
recognize, "Shiva lives within me as me."
Muktananda, to have direct spiritual experience
by obtaining Shakti from the Guru
is sadhana.

One-Pointedness

651. That one whose conduct is noble,
who meditates,
who is absorbed in devotion to the Guru,
obtains glory in this world.

652. Muktananda,
only when you become the Guru
by merging with him
will you understand service to the Guru,
meditation on the Guru,
the Guru's knowledge,
and Guru's grace.

Surrender

653. A loyal wife
is one who has completely lost herself
in her husband.
A disciple becomes perfect
only when he has completely surrendered
to the Guru.

654. When a drop of water falls into the ocean,
it ceases to be a drop
and becomes the whole ocean.
If a man gives himself to the Guru
and then takes himself back,
what kind of disciple is he?

655. Any imperfections that exist in a disciple
are due to self-deception.
Self-deception is surreptitiously holding back,
not giving all, but saying, "I have given.
Why haven't I realized anything?"

Surrender

656. You are without perfect love for the Guru.
His abode is not sacred to you.
You do not listen to his commands.
Muktananda, what kind of disciple are you?
You are nothing but a beggar.

657. While the disciple does not surrender,
his mind cannot become steady.

658. Muktananda,
as long as you cannot obey authority
you cannot command.
Only when you can really obey
can you command.

659. A disciple should surrender completely,
as befits a disciple.
When all the tendencies
toward egoism and separateness
have been consumed in the fire
of the Guru's rule,
only bliss remains.

Disciple

660. Surrender is complete
only when there remains nothing of oneself
to stand in the way.

661. Muktananda,
a perfect disciple renounces his own cleverness,
lives according to Sri Guru's commands,
loves his Guru in thought, word, and deed,
considers his Guru to be God,
and knows no other God.

662. A perfect disciple
gives his mind to Sri Guru's teachings,
joins his heart to his Guru's
and, by surrendering everything,
merges himself in the Guru.

663. You cannot gain all the Guru's wealth
unless you possess a disciple's qualities.
Surrender yourself to Sri Guru,
then you will become the Guru.

Surrender

664. When a disciple completely surrenders
to the Guru,
his reward is total identity with the Guru.

665. The disciple who offers himself to the Guru
and gets Sri Guru fully in return,
attains the state of Nityananda,
the highest realization,
complete self-fulfillment.

666. The disciple
who gives himself completely to Sri Guru
becomes Sri Guru.
Muktananda,
renounce everything and serve Sri Guru.

667. When a disciple surrenders completely,
though still a disciple,
he becomes the Guru.
When a disciple becomes a perfect disciple,
he attains the Guru in his fullness.

Devotion

668. The Guru is truth.
The Guru is everlasting.
The Guru is love.
The Guru is immortal.
Muktananda,
drink deep of the Guru's love
and become deathless.

669. As a sandalwood tree
makes the nearby trees fragrant,
so the Guru
makes his disciple equal to himself.
Muktananda,
offer all your love to the Guru.

670. Sri Guru is Mahadeva.
Ganeshpuri is the Kailas of Parashiva.
Sri Guru's mantra is the mahamantra.
Muktananda, a life of obedience
to the Guru's command
is great loyalty, great devotion.

Devotion

671. To receive when the Guru gives,
to give when the Guru accepts,
to live as the Guru's entirely—
these are the marks
of devotion to the Guru.

672. If devotion is without discipline,
without discrimination in everyday life,
without sensitivity towards others,
it is barren.

673. Rules and restraints
are nothing but discipline.
Self-willed and unrestrained behavior
is not devotion.
Love springs from devotion,
and by love
man becomes disciplined.

XI. LAND OF YOGA

Ganeshpuri

674. Ganeshpuri is blessed
with the grace of Nityananda.
It is paradise on earth.
It is the abode of yogashakti.
Muktananda, it is the Siddhaloka of the earth.

675. Muktananda, you received your body
because of past merit.
You came to Ganeshpuri's sacred region,
Nityananda's Siddhaloka,
his paradise on earth.
If arrogance, obtuseness, or egoism
drive you away
you will lose everything.
You will be unfortunate if you go.

Ganeshpuri

676. Through past merit and great tapasya
you obtained your body.
Through this you came
to the purity of Ganeshpuri.
Live here with steadfastness,
renunciation, and love.
Be truly worthy.

677. Muktananda, you live in the kingdom
where Nityananda is king.
You live in a divine loka.
How can you have a taste
for the loka of poverty?

678. In Ganeshpuri every particle
is saturated with Goddess Chiti Kundalini.
Her luster sparkles and shimmers.
Muktananda, who would wander
in the joyless world,
leaving behind this Chitiloka,
this paradise on earth?

679. Inner nectar contains all contentment.
Discover it.
Ganeshpuri is revealed there.
Muktananda, if you leave this heaven,
where will you go to repent?

680. Chiti Shakti revels in Ganeshpuri,
this paradise on earth.
Muktananda, do not see it
with an evil mind.
See with Chiti,
the gift of Nityananda.

Ashram Dharma

681. You may live in an ashram or at home.
At home you may be a master or a servant,
but at the ashram
you must follow ashram dharma.

682. The one who does not follow ashram dharma
gets no respect in an ashram,
even if he is trustworthy.

683. Ashramites, do nothing
that will spoil the purity
and cleanliness of the ashram.
Here you will realize Brahman
by the power of yoga.

684. If an ashram does not treat all castes equally,
what can you learn there?
The sense of 'I' and 'thou'?

685. In an ashram the illusions of caste,
family, and clan are not found.
An ashram worships friendship for all.

686. To meditate,
to spread meditation,
to live in meditation —
this is the life of the ashram.
In the loka of meditation
what is given is the bliss of meditation
and what is received is the same bliss.

687. Kings saw Sri Rama as a king.
The brave saw Him as brave.
The righteous saw Him as righteous.
The enlightened saw Him as
the Supreme Person.
To the sinful He was an enemy.
The wicked washerman with his wicked heart
saw Him as full of wickedness,
for the sins of the heart are seen outside.
See the ashram as filled with Consciousness.

Ashram Dharma

688. What day is to the blind,
      music to the deaf,
      sweet delicacies to a man
      with a weak stomach,
      Muktananda, the same is this ashram
      to an impure heart.

689. Muktananda, what happiness can you find
      even in heaven, if you have no love,
      if your heart is not clean, your actions not pure?

690. You may live in the sacred region
      of a Siddha
      or move in the company
      of the lords of yoga.
      You may sit in the seat of the powerful
      or enter the temple of meditation.
      A wicked heart sees its own self
      everywhere.

691. Contemplation of sin,
reflection on impurities,
notions of evil and of difference—
Muktananda,
these make one see hell
even in a Siddha's abode.

692. To the blind, light is darkness.
To the deaf, talk is soundless.
To the empty-hearted,
the world is desolate.
Muktananda, to a seer of sin
even Vaikuntha is hell.

693. You can go east or west,
to a city of poverty, to a city of wealth.
Wherever you go
you take yourself with you.

694. Freedom to act without restraint
is the freedom of wild beasts.
Muktananda, in Sri Guru's house
obedience and submission are
supreme freedom.

Ashram Dharma

695. In a religious place
or a house of swadhyaya,
status and title are irrelevant.
Status depends on the difference of function,
while swadhyaya relates to the Self.
The Self is beyond differences.

696. In the world, family tradition
need not be an obstacle.
In spiritual life, you have only
to merge with God.

697. The caste distinctions of the world
are not valid in spiritual life.
In a temple or an ashram all are equal.

698. Muktananda,
in an ashram or a holy place,
with the good, the righteous, the wise,
forget that you hold power
as you forget the concerns of waking
during sleep.

Ashram Dharma

699. You will certainly find peace
if you live in an ashram,
even if you engage yourself in action there.
It is needless to wander forever,
to torment yourself with austerities.
Muktananda, meditate.

700. Always repeat, "Sri Gurudeva! Sri Gurudeva!"
The world may say otherwise
but, Muktananda,
your thoughts are your resting place.

701. Your own attitude is your world.
You live the consequences of your actions.
When Sri Guru appears in your thoughts
your love for him
spreads through your world.
You love the ashram.
You love everything.

702. Muktananda, inside the ashram
Sri Guru is in everything.
The atoms of Sri Guru are in the people,
trees, clothes, water, and light.

703. Living in the ashram is a delicate art,
for the ashram is full of Chiti's rays.
Live here respecting everyone.
Muktananda, only then
will you become sinless.

Yajna

704. Perform yajnas
and ask others to do likewise.
Attend yajnas.
Do everything you can
according to your ability.
Service to the people
is the yajna of Janardana.

705. Don't speak ill of yajnas.
Don't obstruct them.
What is the meaning of yajna?
Reflect on it.
The Lord says in the *Gita*:
"All-pervasive Brahman
is always present in yajnas."
A wise man understands
the importance of a yajna.
A wise man is not mad.

706. By inhaling fragrance
you are happy within.
By eating
you appease the gastric fire.
By looking upon beauty
you delight your eyes.
When you praise others,
they are satisfied.
Will not Narayana,
the deity of yajnas,
be gratified through yajnas?

XII. NOBLE LIFE

Control of the Senses

707. Search for your true dear Friend.
      Always with you,
      He will always uphold you.
      Then you will sleep joyfully.
      Why are you so attached to the flesh?
      All flesh is the same.

708. O sadhaka, seek neither bread
      nor cloth nor coins.
      Seek Rama in whom all wealth lies.

709. Don't be afraid of hunger and thirst.
      What is your stomach
      compared to the abundance of the earth?

710. When you are possessed by the senses
      you lose Rama.
      When you are possessed by Rama
      there is no sensuality.

Control of the Senses

711. As rivers surrender
their waters to the sea,
so pleasures are lost
in the peace of the Self.

712. Wherever the eye goes,
see only your Self.
Wherever the mind goes,
see only your Self.
Bondage is nothing but fear.

713. A man may become a leader
or a philanthropist.
He may wield power or guide others.
But Muktananda, unless he is freed
from desire and greed,
his actions will always bring shame.

714. Many temptations, much sorrow,
an absence of peace in wife and home.
Muktananda, are these the marks
of a virtuous man?

715. Revere woman. She is sublime.
But don't lose your radiance
by burning in the fire of attachment to her.

716. Woman is called the mother of all.
She is supremely beloved.
Look on her with reverence —
but from afar.
Woman is a great fire.

717. Whether the senses are active or inactive,
contentment is the same.
Why then can't you transcend the senses
and be content?

718. The man who envies
another's wealth suffers,
not the man who is envied.
Muktananda, remain content
with your own fortune.
Let him who weeps weep.

Control of the Senses

719. A true and valiant hero is steady,
courageous, and discerning.
He does not weep like a coward.

720. By pursuing the senses,
you became the senses.
By pursuing the body,
you became the body.
Caught in pleasure and pain,
you wept.
You failed to transcend the body.

721. My mind was addicted to various things.
Gradually, by great effort,
I gave them all up.
In the end I had only one addiction—
remembrance of Sri Nityananda.

722. When a lump of salt dissolves
in the ocean
it gives up its saltiness
and becomes the ocean.
When identification with the body
is dissolved,
man becomes God.

Brahmacharya

723. Master the senses
and you will be happy.
A sensualist
can never find happiness in the world.

724. By brahmacharya
you can gain everything.
Preserve it carefully.
Can one without vital energy
achieve anything in the world?

725. By virya, poetry;
by virya, joy;
by virya, love;
by virya, Shakti;
by virya, devotion.
So conserve your vital energy,
and it will conserve you.

726. Brahmacharya is great wealth—
the most important thing in life.

Brahmacharya

727. Brahmacharya is tapas.
It is radiance. It is worship.
It is the recitation of sacred texts.
Muktananda,
honor and preserve brahmacharya.

728. From a small drop of semen,
the large body of a man.
From this body countless drops
and countless other bodies are made.
Muktananda, brahmacharya
is even more important than prana.

729. So long as the body has brahmacharya,
it has Shakti.
So long as the body is full of virya,
the mind stays calm.
Muktananda, what would happen to man
without vital energy?

730. It is better to get rid of feces
than it is to get rid of semen.
If you retain waste,
you succumb to disease.
If you retain semen,
your luster and strength increase.
Know this, Muktananda.

731. Girls and boys,
when you have not reached maturity,
what health or happiness can you find
when you destroy your vital fluid?

732. Virya makes man lovable.
It is truly heaven.
Loss of virya is hell.

733. Get married, men and women;
that is good.
But don't foolishly waste the vital energy
given to you by God.
Become married brahmacharis.

Brahmacharya

734. Excessive indulgence in sex,
unnecessary loss of virya—
Muktananda, understand
that this is a truly hellish life.

735. A tree bears fruit in its season
and in its season the earth produces crops.
Abiding by the season is a great virtue.
Observe full brahmacharya—
mate only when the season is right.

736. Camels and oxen abide by the seasons.
Wretched dogs and buffaloes
abide by the seasons.
Tigers and monkeys abide by the seasons.
Should only man become lower than these?

737. If you want to live in happiness,
if you want your sons and daughters
to be principled and righteous,
Muktananda, teach the lesson
of brahmacharya to all.
That culture is great in which
brahmacharya is a great austerity.

738. Where age is not ripe,
where youth is not mature,
where lawful love is not—
Muktananda, there sexual life
is a yajna of the world of death.

739. Perfect self-control leads you to God.
Practice the tapa of self-restraint.

Renunciation

740. Do not renounce the world.
Renounce the illusion of the world.
The Lord of the world
is in the form of the world.

741. I renounced until I had
renounced everything.
I even renounced food and clothes.
When I renounced renunciation,
I found spirituality in worldly life.

742. What in you is yours to renounce?
What sense objects can be enjoyed
that are different from you?
There is no duality in renunciation
and enjoyment.
When Muktananda saw that as an illusion,
he became happy in his heart.

Noble Life

743. I renounced worldly life
as an obstacle on the path.
Having renounced, I wandered fruitlessly.
When Nityananda's grace descended,
the understanding came—
there is perfect spirituality
even in worldly life.

744. There are poets who compose
without God;
their words are lifeless.
There are men who roll their eyes upward,
affecting meditation.
There are men who renounce clothes
to wear bark.
Muktananda, look at them.
Do they have inner peace?

745. Do not practice tapa,
which will not bring you peace.
You can be naked but without inner calm.
You can wear bark but lack tranquility.
You can renounce everything
and still lack peace.

Renunciation

746. A renunciant who cares about
his family status,
who has conceit of learning,
who takes pride in the strength of his
bhaktas or the masses supporting him,
becomes arrogant and falls.

747. Muktananda, you became a brahmin
but did not find Brahman.
You became a yogi
but there was no samadhi.
You became a bhakta
but were not lost in love.
What did you gain?

748. Can you make what is already made?
Can you spoil what is already spoiled?
The Self is pure as it is.
Muktananda, renounce everything.
Live in inner silence.

Noble Life

749.   Muktananda, leave everything when
the time is ripe for renunciation.
When you die,
everything will fall away anyway.
But do not leave your Guru Nityananda.

750.   Muktananda, leave your home,
leave your sect,
leave the tending of your senses.
But do not leave the one
Sri Guru Nityananda.

Reverence

751. According to Vedanta,
     Brahman is everywhere.
     Therefore, have reverence for everyone.
     If a man sees all men equally,
     if he reveres all creatures and all things,
     he needs no other worship.

752. Muktananda,
     observe the vow of reverence toward all,
     because reverence begets friends,
     enhances love, and makes the nectar of bliss
     flow in the heart.

753. To show reverence
     is always a characteristic of the great.
     It is the way of the wise,
     the way of the realized being.
     Be initiated into this practice.

Noble Life

754. Sages and saints revered everyone.
Kings did likewise.
Reverence is the noblest of family traditions.
It is the gateway to the city of liberation.
Muktananda,
make reverence your way of life.

755. From reverence, right understanding;
from reverence, enhanced intelligence.
Reverence is the way of seers
and it leads to the state of pure Selfhood.

756. Reverence is true beauty and divine wealth
because it purifies the mind.
Therefore obtain the treasure of reverence.

757. Worship with reverence,
meditate with reverence,
even bathe with reverence.
It is supreme bliss.

Reverence

758. Act with reverence
and you please God.
Serve with reverence
and your heart becomes completely pure.
Reason with reverence
and you are filled with knowledge.
Muktananda,
if you want to live in happiness,
revere Nityananda.

Self-Effort

759. Although man inevitably encounters
difficulties in life,
if he courageously pursues truth
and righteousness,
he will certainly triumph.

760. Muktananda, complete your sadhana
as quickly as you can.
Do not leave it in the middle.
Without sadhana,
what can you do in the world?

761. For the man who perseveres
with faith and with real effort,
Kailas is not far.

Self-Surrender

762. God and devotee,
Guru and disciple,
husband and wife,
father and son,
friend and friend,
live in peace only through surrender.

763. Even in worldly life
there is no love, no peace,
without surrender.
Everyone should live
in a state of surrender.
Surrender is the greatest treasure.

764. When a wife surrenders to her husband
in dharma,
he surrenders himself to her.
Reverence and friendliness grow
between them.

765. Through surrender life is filled
with sweetness and a new inspiration.
Learn to surrender.

766. God will surrender Himself to us
exactly as we surrender to Him
and in the same degree.
Learn total surrender.

767. Each petal of the heart lotus
is endowed with
a great and beneficial power.
Muktananda, acquire that power
through surrender in meditation.

768. It is surrender that brings progress,
even in meditation.
Muktananda, self-surrender
is the highest wealth.

XIII. PITFALLS

PITFALLS

Bad Company

769.   The influence of company is strong.
Iron becomes gold
in the company of the philosopher's stone.
Muktananda, do not seek
the company of the degraded.

770.   To play with fire,
to befriend a snake,
to live with a wild beast—
these are safer, Muktananda,
than the company of a degraded man.

771.   By seeing and listening to a holy soul
one's heart is purified.
In the evil company of an evil man
one has to suffer hell.

772.   What if an ass bathes in the Ganges?
What if a rogue becomes a pilgrim?
They will still sing their own tunes.

Bad Company

773. From company, heaven.
From company, hell.
From company, high or low actions.
Muktananda, fear evil company.

774. Always keep away from bad company.
Otherwise the heaven created by your virtues
will be consumed.

775. The fire of wood
burns the body of one lifetime.
But the fire of bad company
burns you through many lifetimes.

PITFALLS

Those Who Use Yoga for Unworthy Ends

776. If a yogi violates the principles of yoga
and takes to worldly ways
to please other people, he wins only scorn.

777. He can be known as an emperor of yoga,
as a perfect master of yoga,
but if, to please sensual and unworthy people,
he compromises yoga
and becomes a slave of pleasure-seekers,
he is hopelessly deluded, completely misled—
though he may call himself
the primal rishi of all maharishis.

778. If a yogi ceases to worship
the eight limbs of yoga,
gives up dharana, dhyana, and samadhi,
and instead becomes a worshiper
of entertainers and celebrities,
he has fallen as far as he can fall—
though he may be known
as the master of all yogas
and the lord of all lords.

Those Who Use Yoga for Unworthy Ends

779. If a yogi abandons worship of the pure yoga
and begins to see dancers,
actors, and actresses in his meditation,
is he worthy of the status of yogi?

780. One who is without reverence for the mantra,
faith in the Guru and love for the Lord—
is such a one a yogi?
Is he anything more than a circus acrobat?

781. If a yogi does not completely accept
the truth of the Vedas,
does not have unquestioning faith
in yajnas and other sacrifices,
and is without respect for the divine Name,
is he worthy of being called a yogi?

782. Anyone who fails to see the greatness
of karma yoga, bhakti yoga, jnana yoga,
mantra yoga, laya yoga, hatha yoga,
raja yoga, yajna yoga, is surely afflicted
by limited understanding and capacity.

PITFALLS

783. Whatever the seers said
after they had attained divine intelligence
is completely true.
They did great good without motive.
Who but an ignorant fool would doubt it?
Certainly a wise man would not.

784. To fall from the path
and still call yourself the most perfect yogi,
the greatest knower of yoga in the world,
and to proclaim, "No one but Krishna
has the knowledge I have"... What madness!

785. Yoga confers infinite capacity,
limitless Shakti,
and deeply blissful transcendental peace.
One who compromises his disciplines
to pursue crazy actors
is not even a convincing actor of yoga,
let alone a yogi.

Those Who Use Yoga for Unworthy Ends

786. A prostitute spends her life
 selling her flesh to earn a living.
 She is better than the yogi
 who uses yoga to earn a name, position,
 endless worldly pleasures, or a large fortune.

787. Horses and oxen eat copiously.
 A camel eats still more.
 An elephant eats half a ton of food a day.
 All fill their stomachs easily.
 Muktananda, why should anyone sell yoga
 for a stomach that requires half a kilo of food?

788. There are many large fish in the ocean.
 They need much food,
 and by God's grace they eat easily.
 A man needs only half a kilo of food.
 Why should he use the power of yoga
 to fill his stomach?

789. Yoga is to be given freely and out of charity.
 Yoga is to bless with grace.
 Yoga is to be taught through compassion.
 When the seers gave yoga to the world,
 they gave without motive.

PITFALLS

790. In the threefold samyama of yoga,
a yogi has everything.
Why should he accumulate external objects?

791. A yogi has everything
if he has the power of yoga.
Yoga is perfect and has all the qualities.
It is free and completely independent.

792. A yogi's body is healthy,
his conduct is healthy,
his life is healthy.
A yogi is universal and supremely free.

793. Muktananda,
only when you attain the highest yoga
will your freedom be absolute.

794. Know it for the truth—
they are not yogis
who have not gained complete freedom,
who every moment are slaves
of their senses, their mind, their actions,
and other people.

Siddhis

795. Muktananda, don't indulge
in wanton display,
don't exhibit siddhis,
don't entice the innocent public.

796. Various arts and entertainments
have been devised to fascinate men's minds,
such as the enchanting movements of actresses,
the songs sung by singers.
Miracles are in the same category.

797. Compared to the siddhi that sustains life
and has some meaning and purpose,
what is the use of siddhis
that are pointless
and are simply performed for show?

798. A siddhi that is useless,
that is beneficial to no one,
that does not help the poor and hungry,
is surely no better than a castle in the air —
even if it is concrete and visible.

PITFALLS

799. Horns seen on a hare,
a snake seen in a rope,
flowers made of air,
the son of a barren woman—
such illusions,
though seeming real,
serve no purpose.
In this universe
that is made in God's image,
fake riddhis and siddhis
are just as futile.

800. A siddhi performed for show,
a forged note,
the marriage of a barren woman's son,
a courtesan depicted in a painting,
who ever got pleasure from these?

801. The siddhi of a farmer is to be admired.
He grows food and so sustains
our life and happiness.

802. Those miracles that keep you far from God—
O renunciants,
how can you be so deluded by them?

Siddhis

803. Everything is unreal but Brahman.
What is visible perishes.
Why become as deluded as a lunatic?

804. O renunciant,
become completely true to your Self.
Keep seeing your own inner miracles.
Then all siddhis will open their doors to you.
You won't have to exhaust yourself
endlessly performing miracles.

805. The magician's alluring miracles
are bestial.
Keep far from them.

806. Where dealings are absolutely honest,
actions absolutely good,
and renunciants absolutely pure—
O Muktananda,
all siddhis dance in attendance there.

PITFALLS

807. Where there is peace within,
    calm and ease without,
    and all activities are free from anxiety,
    there the perfect siddhi dwells.

808. Perfect knowledge of Brahman,
    complete skill in yoga,
    ease in the art of giving instruction,
    ease in action—these, Muktananda
    are the divine siddhis.

809. He who has transcended the senses,
    who eats frugally,
    who continually dwells in the inner Self
    and is lost in devotion to his Guru—
    Muktananda, riddhis and siddhis
    stand before him with folded hands.

810. Any display
    that does not produce detachment of mind,
    any miracle
    that lacks the joy of the Self,
    any action
    that has no use in life,
    is nothing but a child's game.

Siddhis

811. The splendor of a phantom king,
marriage to a woman in a portrait,
ostentatious siddhis... all are alike.
In worldly life, too, everything is useless
that does not embody God's Shakti.

812. For eating, grains grown from the earth;
for drinking, water from the river;
for living, a sharp intellect.
Can an intelligent man find significance
in the miracles that appear and vanish
like a shadow on a screen?

813. Drink, magic, the races, gambling...
the display of siddhis
is an addiction like these.

814. Many grains grow
from one grain of wheat
sown in the earth,
many fruits from one fruit,
many coconuts from one coconut.
Compared to such real and natural siddhis,
what reality is there in ostentatious miracles?

PITFALLS

815.   A crow flying in the sky,
        a fish swimming in water,
        a mustard seed producing many seeds—
        are these not natural siddhis?

816.   From one drop of semen
        man makes a man like himself.
        Plants and fruit trees
        draw sweet sap from the same earth.
        A cow eats blades of grass
        and yields white milk.
        The materialization of ash
        is meaningless compared with these siddhis.

817.   God is the bountiful giver
        of riddhis and siddhis.
        The eight great siddhis
        and the nine riddhis
        are constantly engaged in serving Him.
        Muktananda, which one then
        will forsake Him for you?

818.   The only siddhi worthy of man's attainment
        is the vision of the inner Self.

Siddhis

819. He who has nothing left to attain,
who is beyond sadhana,
whose dwelling place is himself—
what use does he have for a miracle?

820. Where ordinary consciousness
has been transcended
and where awareness of the world,
and of mine and thine, no longer exists,
but where, instead,
there is total immersion in the Self—
Muktananda, there
a siddhi is not even worth a glance.

821. In that supra-transcendental state of oneness
where currents of heavenly bliss flow,
in that state of perfection
where all imperfections dissolve—
Muktananda, why would you seek
a paltry siddhi there?

PITFALLS

822. Where the heart overflows
with the contentment of the Self,
where awareness of the one Self is constant,
where one delights in nothing but the Self—
Muktananda, isn't a siddhi a mirage there?

823. To attain the supreme Lord,
the highest siddhi,
and not to attain perfect tranquility—
can such a state be possible?

XIV. The World Is God

Look upon Everyone as Divine

824. Recognize your universal family.
Every man in the world is your brother.
Why burn with attachment and hatred?
Muktananda, join the family of Vasudeva.

825. The Self is pure, noble, the same in all.
It is without taint.
Muktananda,
why impose upon the great Self
the petty differences of ritual and action?

826. The slaves of ritual reap hardship.
Likewise the high priests of dogma.
For them there can be no contentment.
Muktananda, when you see the sky-blue god
in the center of the sahasrara,
you will understand.
The peace and freedom there
heal all differences.

The World Is God

827. Rama lives in all bodies.
Why do you thrive on conflicts?
When you are conscious of equality
you sip the nectar of peace.

828. The races and religions of man,
Hindu, Moslem, and all the rest,
are one in the court of Rama.
Muktananda, why are you driven
by religious bigotry
to fight and kill for nothing?

829. God's prices are the same for everyone.
Food, water, air, and light
are equally available to all.
The earth sustains all equally.
Muktananda, you sin against your Master
by fighting sectarian battles.

830. Do not get trapped
in religious controversies.
Meditation on the Self
is perfect religion.
Meditate.

Look upon Everyone as Divine

831. Don't waste time debating differences
of caste, sect, and belief;
don't embroil yourself in controversies
about what is high and what is low.
All religions come from the same Rama.

832. A sect is simply a path.
The temple lies beyond it—enter that.
If you don't leave the path,
how will you enter the temple?

833. The whole world burns with jealousy.
It exists among nations, races, and individuals.
Muktananda, where is duality
when the one Lord pervades everything?

834. The only reliable spiritual guides
are the great souls
who have transcended caste,
nation, and language.

The World Is God

835. When I received the Sadguru's grace
I understood that everyone in the universe
shared the same reality.
The distinction between
'my own people' and 'other people'
vanished.

836. India and Pakistan,
America and France,
Europe and Russia,
China and Japan—
the whole world is Narayana's.
Why do you distinguish
between East and West?

837. All nations and societies are noble,
all individuals are noble.
Muktananda, become noble and see.

Look upon Everyone as Divine

838. Unity and diversity
      are man's creation.
      Differences of religion
      are man's creation.
      High and low
      are man's creation.
      Hindus, Moslems, and Christians
      are man's creation.
      Muktananda, God's religion
      is the consciousness of equality
      that we express in our lives.

839. As Rama lives in you,
      so He lives in everyone.
      Treat all with love and equality.
      Equality-consciousness is God's yajna.

840. A dog remains a dog
      even on reaching Kailas.
      A crow remains a crow
      even in Vaikuntha.
      In heaven a pig is a pig.
      Muktananda,
      one who lives in equality-consciousness
      remains there
      even in disagreeable circumstances.

The World Is God

841. If you want happiness, see the equality
that underlies this strange unequal world.
If you want peace, do not accept inequality.
Equality is heaven.
Inequality is hell.

842. We are worshipers of inner bliss
whether you praise us or disparage us.
Muktananda, the bliss of the heart wells up
only in equality-consciousness.

843. People speak of high and low
in the human body.
Both mouth and anus
are parts of the same body.
They are equal.

844. Have affection for everyone.
Affection for man
is a part of devotion to God.

845. Sages and saints appear in all countries,
all religions, all ages.
Their goal is the same.

Look upon Everyone as Divine

846. The wealth of India is in her great souls,
in the saints and sages who are universal.

847. Look upon everyone as divine.
The same one, Sri Guru Nityananda,
lives in man and woman.
He lives in all.

848. Man is woman,
woman is man.
Man and woman are immortal creations
of the same five elements.
Seeing both within yourself,
give up duality.
Be drunk with bliss.

849. Because you lacked Self-knowledge
you saw one as a friend,
another as an enemy,
a third as a stranger.
Muktananda, see your Self.
All are part of your family.

The Many Are One

850. The world that God made
has no attachment or aversion, no duality.
It is always the same,
revolving in the same way,
following the same law,
revealing the same pattern.
Look upon the world
with a vision of its equality.

851. That which was real was perfect.
It was only One,
perfect in its aloneness.
There was no room for another,
because the One was entirely complete.
The perfect did not change its oneness
even when embodied as the many.
Muktananda, That is not two.

852. The real does not give birth to the unreal:
mangoes don't grow on coconut trees;
a cow is not born of a mare.
Muktananda, the world is Truth,
Consciousness, and Bliss.

The Many Are One

853. When the invisible Person thought,
He became man and woman.
As both husband and wife,
He performs all the functions of the world.
Muktananda, behold your Nityananda in both.

854. The dance of Shiva-Shakti
is the world dance of man-woman.
If you observe with discrimination,
you will see no man, no woman,
but only Nityananda.
He is the complete truth.

855. Who had greater manliness
than Gargi, a knower of Brahman,
than Maitreyi, a seeker of the truth,
than the supremely loyal Savitri,
than Yogini Muktabai,
or than the Self-realized Lalleshwari?

The World Is God

856. Understand that the differences
that appear in daily life
are only apparent.
Bracelet, bangle, ring, earring, necklace,
are all made of the same gold,
though their appearances differ.

857. In a blacksmith's workshop,
hammers, tongs, nails, latches, bolts
are made from the same iron.
They are made in different ways
and appear to be different,
but the basic substance is one — iron.

858. Muktananda, see the same cotton
constituting threads and fibers,
cloth, quilts, and sheets.

859. Moksha, jnana, bhakti,
Kailas, Parashiva, and Nityananda —
these many are one.
They all refer to the same state.

The Many Are One

860. Mother, wife, daughter, servant, master—
Muktananda, all are projections
of the one Narayana.

861. Father, son, mother, Guru, disciple—
all are the manifested compassion
of the compassionate One.
Give up name and form
and you will see what remains—
the unchanging soul.

Equality-Consciousness

862. Be aware continually
of the equality of all things.
Equality-consciousness is Rama Himself.
Earn the divine wealth
of seeing equality at every moment.
The continual awareness
of basic and underlying equality
is the divine viewpoint.

863. One who views all things as equal
lives in Rama.
Such equality-consciousness
is the highest attainment of a yogi.
Perfect happiness resides in it.
It is the essence of samadhi.
Muktananda, equality-consciousness
is perfect Brahman; it is Nityananda.

Equality-Consciousness

864. Consciousness of the essential equality
of all things
destroys all feeling of separateness.
When the habit of making distinctions
is destroyed, steadiness of mind arises,
and from this comes the immutable state.
It is this state that is worth attaining.

865. From equality-consciousness,
one-pointedness,
and from one-pointedness,
a blissful mind.
Only a mind filled with bliss
knows perfection.
So first become aware that all things
are essentially equal.

866. The equality of all things
is the Rama of Ayodhya Himself.
It is the Shyam of Gokul.
It is the blue-throated Shiva.
Muktananda, do japa of equality
ceaselessly.

867. Equality-consciousness is perfect wisdom
and is the yajna that gives the desired fruit.
Attain it — that is the command of Nityananda.

868. Always live in equality-consciousness.
It is the well-protected and civilized city.
Bathe in equality-consciousness;
all your impurities will be washed away.
Be consumed in its fire;
all your sins will be burned away.
Equality-consciousness
and Nityananda are one:
the ocean of immortality.
Drink deeply of its nectar
and become deathless.

869. Attain equality-consciousness
because God dwells there.
Your peace is there.
Yogis, bhaktas, and jnanis all rest there.
Leave disharmony forever.
Equality-consciousness is supreme harmony,
is Sri Guru Nityananda,
is the highest truth.

Equality-Consciousness

870. The mantra arises, the mind merges,
the universe of an individual
is born, sustained, and dissolved
in equality-consciousness,
because that is the true nature of Nityananda.

871. Attain equality-consciousness
and you will become happy.
Without it,
all is disharmony and insensitivity.

God's Caste

872. Before your birth, caste was not there,
and it will not be there after your death.
Caste cannot be found
in any part of the body, in any limb.
Muktananda, you are far from caste.

873. If caste, family, and clan
can be used to help you recognize
the basic truth,
they have meaning.
The supreme Being is the fundamental caste.

874. If through caste, family, and convention
you are obstructed
then, Muktananda, are they not chains?

875. Sannyasa is the renunciation
of all castes and actions.
Sannyasa has no limitations.
It states "I am Brahman."
Muktananda, caste is limited.

God's Caste

876. Look at the body—
right from that of Brahma
to that of an insect,
each is made up of five elements.
Prana causes hunger and thirst in each.
Each has a mind.
Muktananda,
if you were to look inward,
you would see that the Self,
and only the Self, is all-pervasive.

877. God who is casteless
and free from all attributes
became the five elements.
Muktananda,
where then does caste come from?

878. The body is made up of five elements,
and that is the caste of the body.
Brahman became individual consciousness,
and that is the caste of the soul.
Tell me Muktananda,
what other caste can there be?

The World Is God

879. God is love. God is morality. God is caste.
Muktananda, join God's caste
and become happy.

880. Heaven and hell are beyond caste.
Hari, Hara, and Brahma are beyond caste.
Sacred places are beyond caste.
Muktananda, where did you see caste
in the inner Self?

881. Do not mislead others
by saying that caste is religion.
Muktananda, what is the caste
of Parashiva?

882. Caste distinctions
are distinctions of high and low.
God transcends them.
If you want peace,
you must transcend caste.

God's Caste

883. Caste and family traditions
are related only to the body.
What else but meditation can take you
to the blue firmament beyond the body?

884. A statue made of clay,
hands of clay, feet of clay,
mouth, trunk, eyes—
all of clay.
Muktananda, when you see your body as this,
your delusion will disappear.

885. In contentment there is no caste distinction.
In peace all creeds and sects are one.
In all nations contentment is one.
You will find it through meditation.
Muktananda, what is the use of a path
that does not lead to peace?

886. The four castes
are from the One without caste.
From one, four castes.
One in all the four.
Muktananda, all castes
are of the one Self.

Play of Reality

887. It is essential to see with oneness,
even in worldly life
that is full of duality.
Oneness alone is the sign of yoga.
Eyes see, ears hear, tongue speaks,
yet they are all one;
they all belong to the same body.

888. Seeing differences,
behaving with partiality,
thinking in terms of high and low—
these destroy the inner state.
Oneness is the state that gives bliss.

889. The head of a large family
knows the entire family is his.
All the members of the family,
though many, have come from the one.
It is the same with the universal family
of the supreme Lord, Vasudeva.

Play of Reality

890. Muktananda, as long as you have no awareness
of the one family of Vasudeva,
and don't practice
universal brotherhood and love,
the world cannot be happy.

891. While there was 'I,'
I could not see Rama.
But after all that I thought was mine
was consumed in the fire of knowledge
that was fanned by meditation,
I saw Rama and only Rama.

892. Though he has ears,
a deaf man does not hear.
Even by daylight,
a blind man cannot see.
A man who is dumb cannot speak,
though he has a tongue.
In the same way, Muktananda,
one who has received the Guru's grace
sees nothing earthly in the universe.

The World Is God

893. Inner peace, serenity,
the ending of the sense of duality,
the transcendence of thought—
that, indeed, is freedom from the world,
Muktananda, that is realization.

894. Only one Self plays
in the whole company
of men and women in the world.
There is no other.

895. Overcome all thoughts
and see what appears within you.
Multiplicity is only a concept—
the perfect reality is one.

896. What has emerged from reality
is not different from reality,
is contained in reality,
is itself reality.
Muktananda,
whatever you see is also reality.
And awareness of your own Self
is the supreme Reality.

Play of Reality

897. The four categories of physical form—
those born from an egg, from sweat, from seed,
and from the womb,
the human body included—
are all combinations, in varied proportions,
of the five elements.
The five elements are in turn
divided into twenty-five portions.
Muktananda, in everything
there is this same play
of five and twenty-five.

898. Don't see the objective world as alien.
It is the very garden of Nityananda,
the open school of Vedanta.
Learn here. Pass the examinations
and receive your degree.

899. This human world
is the family of the one supreme Father
and the one imperishable Mother.
While man does not learn to worship
this state of knowledge,
his weeping will not cease.

The World Is God

900.   Duality lives in attachment,
desire, and jealousy.
The illusion of separateness
feeds ignorance.
Muktananda, to see another as a stranger
is to live in a house of sorrow.
Peace is far from there.

901.   A painter uses one set of colors
and one brush to paint many pictures.
Likewise, man and woman
spring from the one Being.
They are different, yet one.
There is neither high nor low.

902.   Man and woman
are made from the same five elements.
Only outwardly do they differ.
To the jnani,
there is no difference between them.

903.   The undifferentiated dance of Shiva-Shakti
is the very essence of man and woman.
Muktananda, don't see man-woman as two.

Play of Reality

904. Duality is only stupidity.
Duality is sanctioned neither by the scriptures
nor humanity nor ethics.
The cult of duality
is the cult of hell on earth.

905. God is one. His vision is one.
His progeny is one.
In Him there is no sense of duality,
no higher or lower.
Muktananda, to see many in that One
is the mahamantra of death.

906. Difference of one country from another,
of one language from another,
of one sect from another,
difference created by name and form—
Muktananda, these are all the pits
of the yajna of hell.

The World Is God

907.   The vast earth, one;
the flowing water, one;
the moving air, one;
the spreading ether, one;
the conscious Self, the basis of all,
supremely blissful, one.
Muktananda, tell me, where is other?

Guru's Eye

908. The Lord of the universe in the universe,
and you in the Lord of the universe.
There is only one, Muktananda—
in innumerable forms.

909. One is infinite.
In the infinite is one.
In all is the unfolding of one.
Muktananda, what else is there
when nothing else is?

910. Ghee is not separate from butter.
Oil is not separate from the seed.
God is not separate from the world.
Muktananda, annihilate your separateness
and see what the world is.

The World Is God

911.   Muktananda,
       threads, cloth.
       Bracelets, gold.
       Anklets, silver.
       Pitchers, clay.
       Man and the universe, Nityananda.

912.   The universe exists
       in the pervasiveness of the One.
       Man, give up your sense of differences.
       Worship Nityananda in all.

913.   Muktananda,
       the supreme God
       is the ground of the universe.
       Here the Self is revealed,
       expanded, supreme.
       See with the Guru's eye.

914.   Because you do not see things as they are,
       because of duality in your mind
       and a perverse understanding,
       Muktananda, you, the One,
       appear to be many.

915. While your understanding is imperfect,
maya, jiva, and God seem different.
When your understanding is perfect,
you will see the world
as the blissful drama of God.

916. The Self plays in high and low;
the Self is a king,
the Self is a beggar.
A king becomes a beggar,
a beggar becomes a king.
Muktananda, the play goes on.

917. One became two.
The non-dual became dual.
The pure Being, Satchidananda,
became the cosmos.
Muktananda, do not get caught
in conflicts of acceptance and rejection.
The One and the many are the same.
Be calm.

918. 'Inward-turning mind'
and 'outgoing mind'
are scriptural concepts
that have no reality.
That which is fully inside
is also fully outside.

919. The distinction between 'inward-turning'
and 'outgoing' is an obstruction.
To understand the meaning of the scriptures
you need direct experience.

920. Don't consider yourself great
by seeing others as small.
Don't think that you know Brahman
when you make a distinction
between matter and consciousness.
Muktananda, all is one.
Consciousness appears as matter
just as water takes the form of ice.

921. Muktananda, you imagine virtue and sin
through ignorance,
as a child imagines
that a post is a thief.

Guru's Eye

922. Do not defile your heart
by seeing God's world as impure.
The Lord of the universe
is in the form of the universe.
That which you see as impure is pure.

923. The universe that appears in God
exists in God as God.
Muktananda, you are His.

XV. BLUE LIGHT

Blue Light

924. In the glowing center of the heart,
blue light shines.
Bathe in the pure blue rays.
Muktananda, the external is without joy.

925. See the gleaming center of the 72 million nadis.
See the blue radiance.
Muktananda, why do you desire greatness
in the impure, lusterless world?

926. The brilliance of the world,
the exuberance of the strong,
the glow of a beautiful face,
the rhythm of true poetry—
all are pitch-black night
without the light of the Blue.

927. In the light of the blue jewel
the poor become rich and the joyless joyful.
The ignorant are filled with knowledge
and virtue grows where before there was none.

Blue Light

928.   From there, there is no return.
       It is the land of no weeping,
       the home of prosperity.
       Muktananda, that is the blue light
       of eternal Consciousness.

929.   In the conscious temple of light,
       in the sahasrara,
       dwells your beloved blue jewel.
       Find it through meditation.

930.   In the center of the upper space
       the Blue Pearl waits.
       It is as small as a sesame seed
       and shimmers in the inner air.
       O Muktananda,
       where else is your journey directed?

931.   See the luminous inner light.
       How full of nectar it is!
       The blue light is the light of the Self.

Blue Light

932.   The Blue Pearl is pure,
        all-knowing, of tremendous speed.
        It contains the supreme God.
        Muktananda, you renounced the world
        to find That.
        Why do you wander from forest to forest?

933.   The forms of Hari and Hara
        appear and disappear
        in the blue light of Consciousness.
        Muktananda, you think you know everything
        and yet you don't know That.

934.   He appears to be small but is boundless.
        He is a tiny particle and the whole cosmos as well.
        He is your own but belongs to everyone.
        Muktananda, sometime,
        make that Blue God your friend.

Blue Light

935. That is your friend
though you may not know it.
That is your protector
though you may not accept it.
That is your life
though you may not understand it.
Muktananda, why did you spurn That?
You still have not reached
the radiant Consciousness
beyond the Blue.

936. The inner Consciousness
is smaller than small,
larger than large.
It is pure even amidst impurity
and equally present in all.
Muktananda, everyone belongs to it.

937. Do not delude others by saying,
"God does not exist because we do not see Him."
Muktananda, see in the center of the sahasrara.
God is fully manifested there.

Blue Light

938. The Blue God pervades the six chakras.
He reigns from muladhara's center
to the center of sahasrara's sky.
He creates. He sustains. He dissolves.
Behold his beauty.
All human happiness is there.

939. Those who see the Blue Pearl,
the light blazing through sahasrara's sun,
are the most blessed.

940. The Blue Spirit
is neither man nor woman,
big nor small.
Muktananda,
it only assumes those forms.
Man and woman spring from it.

941. The Blue Pearl is the ocean
in the form of a drop.
It is the eternal conscious blue light.
It is the home of all the gods,
of Rama, of Krishna.

Blue Light

942.   The rising of yogic realization,
the setting of the illusion of the world,
the attainment of the state of wisdom,
are all caused by the glowing Blue Pearl.

943.   There is bliss in the play of the senses.
From the steadiness of Vedantic wisdom
comes the bliss of Brahman.
In the highest devotion nectar flows.
The bliss of the Blue Pearl is greater
than all these.
It is the most divine.

944.   The untainted blue light
is the pure consciousness of mantra,
the power of the realized yogi,
sublime devotion to the Guru,
the perfect rest for man.

Blue Light

945. When the Blue Goddess reveals herself
there is perfect fulfillment.
The eight-limbed yoga
is consummated in samadhi,
Vedanta is consummated
in right understanding,
the search for truth is consummated
in equality-consciousness.

946. When the Blue God gives his blessing
devotion is filled with ambrosia,
knowledge is filled with bliss,
yoga with the consciousness of equality.

947. In the still radiance of the heart,
in the prophetic visions of Tandraloka,
in the omniscience of Sarvajnaloka,
are the revelations that make man God.

Blue Light

948.   The Blue Pearl is an ocean of joy.
        For jnanis, there is bliss of knowledge,
        for bhaktas, bliss of love,
        for yogis, bliss of yoga.
        Muktananda,
        that eternal conscious blue light
        is Mahadeva among gods.

949.   The goal of philosophy,
        the object of meditation,
        the Rama of Rama,
        the Krishna of Krishna,
        the God of gods,
        Muktananda, that is the inner blue light.

XVI. JIVANMUKTA

Siddha

950. Now listen to the signs
of one who has attained the highest state.
He may not appear to be perfect to the eye,
yet he has reached complete awareness
of the Self.
He is a perfect Siddha.

951. He who is devoid of desire,
having realized God;
he for whom there is nothing else to attain,
who is fulfilled and blessed in himself—
he is indeed a perfect Siddha.

952. He who has seen the universe in himself
and himself in the universe;
who has seen the One
in the animate and the inanimate universe;
he alone is a true Siddha.

Siddha

953. He who annihilated the universe
and also annihilated himself—
Muktananda, that Siddha lived,
he truly lived;
from mortal he became immortal.

954. He who merges himself in God
and God in himself—
he truly sees his own Self.
Muktananda, who is a greater Siddha than he?

955. He who sees Brahman, speaks Brahman,
embodies Brahman,
is worthy of being called Brahman;
he for whom seer, seen, and seeing
are Brahman,
for whom nothing exists
but the perfect, one, non-dual Brahman—
Muktananda, he is a true Siddha.
He is not deluded.

JIVANMUKTA

956. Full awareness of everything,
a calm mind, contentment beyond the senses,
inner sense perception—
all these are the marks of a Siddha.

957. He who is perfect within,
who is absorbed in equality-consciousness
though appearing to be blank, inactive,
and insensitive,
is God-realized and a true Siddha.

958. He who sees the One
within and without,
who sees the One filling all,
whose mind is aware only of the One,
and who has attained the One—
who is a greater Siddha than he?

Jnani

959. Only by becoming a jnani
can you know his state, his wisdom,
his consciousness, Muktananda—
not from afar.

960. A jnani is beyond do's and don'ts.
His way of life is simple and spontaneous
like that of a child.
But while a child is forgetful
of his own nature, a jnani is not.

961. A jnani is perfect Brahman.
How can he be bound by rules,
by the tenets of belief?
He is without name and form.
He revels in the play of his own will.

962. A sleeper cannot see the objective world.
In waking, a man cannot see dreams.
A jnani, in his state of enlightenment,
does not see the universe.

963. Muktananda,
the man who has discarded identification
with the body, with the sense of mine,
is a jivanmukta.
To him blame and praise are mere words.
He is free from desire.
He is a disciplined yogi.

964. Muktananda, that noble soul
who is colored by the color of the Self,
is a jivanmukta.
He lives alone even while living among people.
He lives within himself wherever he goes.

XVII. KNOW YOUR SELF

Yourself and Your Divine Self

965. Having got for yourself
a human birth in this world,
isn't it a waste of effort to do no more
than carry the load of worldliness?

966. Having obtained a human body,
what have you done for the highest good
other than eat, sleep, copulate, and live in fear?
Have you reflected in an objective manner
on why you came into this world?
For you, resting in the Self
has meant worshiping duality—
attachment and aversion,
love and lack of love.

Yourself and Your Divine Self

967. You did not come to know the Self
through a great yearning for liberation.
You did not achieve steadiness of mind
through detachment.
God gave to you without motive,
yet you did not give with an open heart.
You did not strive for liberation,
or study any aspect of yoga,
or acquire devotion.
You never gave up bad company
for satsang with the Siddhas.
How much of your life
have you squandered in vain?

968. What have you earned
since you came into the world?
What discipline have you observed?
Have you known any pleasures greater
than those of germs, insects, birds,
and animals?
Muktananda, you departed as you came.
You have missed your chance to attain
the supreme experience of Nityananda.

Know Your Self

969. How long will you stay sleeping?
When will you wake?
Why do you take pleasure
in the sleep of ignorance?
You weep your whole life through
instead of living free from anxiety.
Why does it please you more to weep
than it does to laugh?
You keep crying and complaining
"Oh, I am dying! Oh, I am dying!"
O foolish mind, give up your restlessness.
Seek contentment in Sadguru Nityananda.

970. You achieved human birth
to become enslaved by greed,
to burn in the fire of anger.
You put your head
between the grinding wheels of samsara.
Taking pride in your own effort,
you learned weeping. Out of laziness,
you gave up good actions.
You gained neither devotion
to the Guru and God,
nor full detachment.
Muktananda, for the glass of samsara,
you have lost the diamond of Self-realization.

Yourself and Your Divine Self

971. Believing the world to be real,
you forgot yourself.
Thus you earned hunger and thirst.
"What I ate yesterday is
what I eat today,
and I will eat the same tomorrow."
Brooding like this, you consumed your heart.
Oh, you did not obey the command
of the Guru or of the scriptures,
you did not seek holy company.
Muktananda, O sleeping one,
now that you have awakened,
clasp the lotus feet of Nityananda.

972. To claim to be a servant of Rama,
to serve as a slave to Sri Money,
and to wander from street to street like a dog—
Muktananda, what sort of holiness is this?

973. It is impossible to spend a long time
with one who is not realized.
Total surrender is made to him
who is realized—
it is impossible to turn away.

Know Your Self

974. If man flatters man to satisfy him,
he will receive only scorn in return.
If he acts to satisfy the supreme Self,
he will become blissful.

975. Move with truth
in the world of the supreme Self.
Remain untainted.
It does not matter
if nobody gives you recognition.
Muktananda, of what use will it be
if even the whole world recognizes you
when Rama does not recognize you?

976. Get to know the supreme Self fully,
and you will get to know everything.
If the Beloved of the heart
is revealed in the heart,
all arts will be revealed to you.

977. Everyone wants to enter into an ideal palace.
Make your own heart ideal.
Why do you wander from door to door?

Yourself and Your Divine Self

978. That which vibrates within
is the same as that which revels without.
Consider within and without to be one.
Muktananda, this is the viewpoint of Shiva.

979. When you obliterate self
you become Self.
Without this, God is far.

980. He Himself is destiny.
He is the mine of good fortune.
This nectarean God
is manifest in the heart.

981. He who does not believe That
to be within himself,
in spite of the effulgent and luminous light
that the Self manifests in the heart,
is surely like a pauper
standing under a wish-fulfilling tree.

Know Your Self

982. Those who say about That, which lives
in the heart, experienced there
by countless pure souls:
"Why do we not experience That?" —
are they not unfortunate?

983. With an intellect that is firm and undoubting,
examine the rules and rituals
framed by our ancient seers.
See whether there is falsity.
Look too upon the stupidities
expounded by the unbelieving,
ignorant, insensitive, hypocritical.
See where truth lies.

984. Know your Self, seek your Self,
delight in your Self. Muktananda, as long
as you don't delight in your Self,
where will you find steadiness?

985. The universe exists because you exist,
God exists because you exist,
dharma exists because you exist.
Muktananda, why do you ignore your Self
and seek other?

986. Muktananda, He who is the seer of dreams
and dwells in the throat
with nineteen subtle mouths
in the dream state,
who lights up countless imaginary
dream worlds in the Void
and sees them—
isn't He the supreme Self?

987. He who, while actually dwelling in the heart
in the supreme Void of deepest sleep,
sees even what is non-existent
as though it were real—
isn't the seer of that state,
devoid of phenomena,
the pure divine Self?

988. The conscious radiance that is to be found
in the emptiness of the supreme space,
in the upper forehead in the sahasrara—
is that not an experience of the Self?
That is, in truth,
the supra-transcendental bliss.

Know Your Self

989. He who is even further than space
and even closer than the heart,
that all-pervasive Rama,
the giver of all things—
He is there in the form of light.

990. That, which is different from activity,
other than matter, beyond the veil,
in which imperishable unbroken light
shimmers eternally—
that very supreme Being is you.
Why then are you always crying and weeping?

991. That by which all states are perceived,
together with mind, intellect, and speech—
is That merely a sense organ?
See the inner great light
which is subtler than the subtlest—
is That just a body?
Oh, why have you left the Knower of all,
the Illuminator of all,
to wander in darkness?

992. That which is seen is all Shiva.
Don't regard anything as different from Shiva.
This universe is the image of its Lord.
Love it. Be devoted to it.
The Lord of the universe
has incarnated Himself as the universe.
See all things as Shiva.
Muktananda, where is the Lord of the universe
apart from the universe?

993. The Seer who is seen through meditation,
the Knower of knowledge,
the Mover of the mind,
the Witness of all that appears,
the Experiencer of all—
Muktananda, That, truly you are,
and That is Sri Nityananda.

Compassionate Sri Nityananda

994. Obtain Sri Guru's blessing.
You will attain peace and happiness.
By Guru's grace
Muktananda acquired the eye
that sees Chiti everywhere.

995. Because you looked at others
you lost your sight.
But, Muktananda, when you saw your Self,
you gained the inner eye.

996. When your viewpoint becomes divine,
you attain Hari.
Muktananda received
the eye of knowledge from the Guru.
It is the only eye in the world
worth having.

997.   Without Chiti's grace,
       without the Guru's eye of knowledge,
       everyone in this world is blind.
       The only one who sees
       is the one who sees himself as God.

998.   When I heard the sweet inner music,
       all other music left me.

999.   I heard several kinds of nada.
       My mind was drunk with bliss.
       Inside myself I found the happiness
       I was looking for outside.

1000. By Guru's grace
       Muktananda heard divine melodies
       in a great effulgence of light
       and was filled to the brim with nectar.

Know Your Self

1001. I attained the knowledge
of the six lotuses.
I saw the glow of all the nadis
and the form of the central nadi.
Seeing that
the sunrise of my good fortune
was within,
I saw my own Self.

1002. I saw heaven and all of hell,
I saw ancestors and Siddhas
and yet another marvel—
I saw Nityananda in the inner blue light.

1003. As a result of your good deeds,
by the blessings of the elders,
by the invisible writing of destiny,
Muktananda, in this body,
in this very birth,
you attained Nityananda as your reward.

1004.   In the crown of the head,
        in the sahasrara,
        the God of gods is seated.
        By Sri Guru's grace
        I found Radhe Shyam within.

1005.   Your own pleasure and delight,
        the object of your love,
        your wealth,
        your beauty,
        your nectar—
        Muktananda, you became all these
        when you received Guru's grace.

1006.   Because of ego I found ignorance.
        Because of ignorance I regarded Chiti's play
        not as Chiti's play, but only as the world.
        And so I began to weep.
        When Nityananda transformed 'I'
        into *So'ham*,
        I perceived the world not as the world,
        but as the play of Consciousness,
        as Goddess Chiti.
        And then I began to laugh and laugh,
        and sing and dance.

1007. Now weeping has wept itself out
and gone away.
Laughter has taken its abode within me
every moment, forever.
For this I must ever repay
the one who is called
compassionate Sadguru Sri Nityananda.

1008. How glad of heart I am.
How much I laugh and dance and leap.
I am immersed in the drunkenness
of transcendental joy.
When Nityananda revealed himself
in my heart,
I attained this state.

This is the inspiration of Goddess Chiti.
There is no poetry, no art, no learning in it.
Muktananda, this is the inner Word,
the gift of Nityananda's grace.

This is a spontaneous,
unbroken vibration of the inner Self
where Nityananda's grace spreads.
Muktananda, this is the vibration of ecstasy.

Guidemap to Holy Sites

GUIDE TO SANSKRIT PRONUNCIATION

VOWELS

Sanskrit vowels are categorized as either long or short. In English transliteration, the long vowels are marked with a bar above the letter and are pronounced twice as long as a short vowel. The vowels "e" and "o" are also pronounced like long vowels.

Short:
- *a* as in c*u*p
- *i* as in g*i*ve
- *u* as in f*u*ll
- *e* as in s*a*ve
- *o* as in ph*o*ne

Long:
- *ā* as in c*a*lm
- *ī* as in s*ee*n
- *ū* as in sch*oo*l
- *ai* as in *ai*sle
- *au* as in c*ow*

CONSONANTS

The main variations from the way consonants are pronounced in English are the aspirated consonants. These are pronounced with a definite *h* sound. In particular, *th* is not pronounced like the English *th* as in *th*rone, nor is *ph* pronounced as in *ph*one. They are pronounced as follows:

- *kh* as in in*kh*orn
- *gh* as in lo*gh*ut
- *jh* as in he*dgeh*og
- *th* as in an*th*ill
- *dh* as in a*dh*ere
- *ph* as in loo*ph*ole
- *bh* as in a*bh*or
- *ñ* as in ca*ny*on
- *sh* as in bu*sh*
- *ksh* as in au*ct*ion

GLOSSARY

72 MILLION NADIS: *See* nadis.

ADHARMA (*adharma*): Lack of righteousness; failure to perform one's proper duty.

AHALYA (*ahalyā*): The wife of the seer Gautama. Because of an infidelity, she was turned into stone by her husband's curse, but recovered her human form when touched by Lord Rama's foot. Her story is told in the *Rāmāyana*.

AHAM BRAHMASMI (*aham brahmāsmi*): (*lit.* "I am Brahman," the supreme Absolute) One of the four great statements (*mahāvākyas*) containing the wisdom of the Upanishads; it occurs in the *Brihadarānyaka Upanishad*, at the end of the *Yajur Veda*.

AJAPA-JAPA (*ajapa-japa*): The natural and effortless repetition of the *mantra* that goes on within every living creature in the form of the incoming and outgoing breath. *See also* So'ham-Hamsa.

AJAPA-NADA (*ajapa-nāda*): The sound of the natural mantra of the breath. *See also* ajapa-japa.

ALAKNANDA (*alakanandā*): A sacred river in the Himalayas.

AMBA (*ambā*): A name of the divine Mother; the beautiful form of Durga. *See also* Durga.

ANNAPURNA (*annapūrnā*): The goddess of food and of abundance.

ANUSHTHANA(S) (*anushthāna*): Ritualistic repetition of a mantra for a set number of times during a given period.

ARATI (*āratī*): A ritual act of worship during which a flame, symbolic of the individual soul, is waved before the form of a

Glossary

deity, sacred being, or image that embodies the divine light of Consciousness. *Āratī* is usually preceded by the sound of bells, conches, and drums, and accompanied by the singing of a prayer.

ARJUNA (*arjuna*): The third of the five Pandava brothers and one of the heroes of the *Mahābhārata*, considered to be the greatest warrior of all. He was the friend and devotee of Lord Krishna. It was to Arjuna that the Lord revealed the knowledge of the *Bhagavad Gītā*. *See also* Mahabharata.

ASHRAM (*āshrama*): (*lit.* a place that removes the fatigue of worldliness) The abode of a Guru or saint; a monastic place of retreat where seekers engage in spiritual practices and study the teachings of *yoga*. *See also* Gurukula.

ASHRAM DHARMA (*āshrama dharma*): Right action in relation to ashram life; the inner posture and outer behavior that allow a person to devote himself or herself to the high attitude and disciplines of ashram life. *See also* dharma; Gurukula.

ATMAN (*ātman*): Divine Consciousness residing in the individual; the supreme Self.

AYODHYA (*ayodhyā*): The birthplace of Lord Rama in north India.

AYURVEDA (*ayurveda*): (*lit.* knowledge of life) The ancient Indian science of medicine, which teaches that good health depends on maintaining the even balance of the three bodily humors: wind, bile, and phlegm.

BADRI, BADRINATH (*badarīnātha*): One of the major centers of pilgrimage in north India, sacred to Lord Vishnu, located in the heart of the Himalayas at about 10,000 feet.

BHAGAWAN (*bhagawān*): (*lit.* the Lord) One endowed with the six attributes or powers of infinity: spiritual power, righteousness, glory, splendor, knowledge, and renunciation. A term of great honor. Swami Muktananda's Guru is known as Bhagawan Nityananda. *See also* Nityananda, Bhagawan.

BHAKTA(S) (*bhakta*): A devotee, a lover of God; a follower of *bhakti yoga*, the path of love and devotion.

BHAKTI (YOGA) (*bhakti*): The path of devotion described by the sage Narada in his *Bhakti Sūtras*; a path to union with the Divine

Glossary

based on the continual offering of love and the constant remembrance of the Lord.

BHARAT-RATNA (*bhārat-ratna*): (*lit.* jewel of India) The highest title of honor awarded by the National Government of India for achievements in the Arts and Humanities.

BHIMA (*bhīma*): The second of the Pandavas and brother of Arjuna. He was known for his immense strength, said to be equal to that of 10,000 elephants. One of the warrior heroes of the epic *Mahābhārata*.

BHULOKA (*bhūloka*): (*lit.* earth world) This world; the earth plane of existence.

BILVA (*bilva*): A tree with medicinal qualities that is sacred to Lord Shiva.

BLUE FIRMAMENT: *See* Blue Pearl.

BLUE GOD (*nīleshwara*): The form that exists within the Blue Pearl; the Lord who grants the final vision to the meditator. Also described by Swami Muktananda in his spiritual autobiography *Play of Consciousness* as "the Blue Person," and in this work as "the Blue Spirit." *See also* Blue Pearl.

BLUE LIGHT: *See* Blue Pearl.

BLUE PEARL (*nīla bindu*): Also referred to as *nīleshwarī*, the Blue Goddess; brilliant blue light, the size of a tiny seed. The subtle abode of the inner Self, and the vehicle by means of which the soul travels from one world to another either in meditation or at the time of death. Swami Muktananda writes extensively about his powerful inner visions of the Blue Pearl in his spiritual autobiography *Play of Consciousness*. *See also* four lights.

BLUE RADIANCE: *See* Blue Pearl.

BLUE SPIRIT: *See* Blue God.

BLUE-THROATED SHIVA (*shiva*): Lord Shiva's throat turned blue from the poison He drank to save the cosmos. The story is told in the *Shiva Purāna*. *See also* Shiva.

BODILY CONSTITUENTS: These are seven according to *Ayurveda,* the ancient Indian science of medicine: blood, bone, fat, flesh, lymphatic fluid, marrow, and semen.

Glossary

BRAHMA (*brahmā*): One of the gods of the Hindu trinity; the creator of the universe.

BRAHMACHARYA (*brahmacharya*): (*lit.* abiding in Brahman, the Absolute; code of conduct based on Brahman) The first of the four stages of life traditional for Hindus, in which a student practices celibacy and is engaged in scriptural study. In the context of these verses, *brahmacharya* means complete celibacy for the unmarried and temperance for people in the second stage of life, married householders.

BRAHMACHARIS (*brahmachāris*): Married householders (people in the second stage of traditional Hindu life), who enjoy sexual union only when the wife is fertile for progeny. This is what is meant by "season-abiding."

BRAHMAN (*brahman*): The supreme Being without form or attributes. *See also* Satchidananda; Upanishads.

BRAHMIN: A scholar, priest, or teacher. *See also* caste.

BRIHASPATI (*brihaspati*): The celebrated Guru of the *devas* (gods).

CASTE: Ancient Indian society was organized into four *varnas*, divisions or castes, for the performance of various functions: *brahmins* were scholars, priests, and preceptors; *kshatriyas* were rulers and warriors; *vaishyas* were businessmen and agricultural workers; *shudras* were menial laborers.

CALCUTTA: A city in West Bengal, India, sacred to the goddess Kali, where the river Ganges reaches the ocean.

CAUSAL BODY: One of the supraphysical bodies; the state of deep sleep occurs here. This body is black in color and the size of a fingertip. *See also* four bodies.

CENTRAL NADI: *See* sushumna.

CHAKRA(S) (*chakra*): (*lit.* wheel) A center of energy located in the subtle body where the *nādīs* converge, giving the appearance of a lotus. Six major *chakras* lie within the *sushumnā nādī*, or central channel. They are: *mūlādhāra* at the base of the spine, *svādhishthāna* at the root of the reproductive organs, *manipūra* at the navel, *anāhata*, the "lotus of the heart," *vishuddha* at the throat, and *ājñā* between the eyebrows. When it is awakened, the *kundalinī* flows upward from the *mūlādhāra* to the seventh

Glossary

chakra, the *sahasrāra*, at the crown of the head. *See also* Kundalini; nadis; shaktipat.

CHATAKA (*chataka*): A mythological bird who drinks nothing but the raindrops falling under a certain constellation; a symbol of absolute loyalty and single-minded devotion.

CHITI, CHITI KUNDALINI, CHITI SHAKTI (*chiti, kundalinī, shakti*): The power of universal Consciousness; the creative aspect of God portrayed as the universal Mother, the Goddess. She is known by many names.

CHITILOKA (*chitiloka*): (*lit.* world of Chiti) The abode of Chiti Shakti. *See also* Chiti.

DAMAYANTI (*damayantī*): The faithful wife of King Nala, who stood by her husband through all his trials and tribulations. Their story is told in the *Mahābhārata*.

DARGAH (*dargah*): The shrine of a Muslim saint.

DARSHAN (*darshan*): (*lit.* to have the sight of; viewing) A glimpse or vision of a saint; being in the presence of a holy being; seeing God or an image of God.

DEVALOKA (*devaloka*): (*lit.* the world of the gods) Heaven; the realm of perpetual youth, delight, and joy.

DHARANA (*dhārana*): Concentration; the sixth stage of *yoga* described by Patanjali in the *Yoga Sūtras*; also, a centering technique described in the *Vijñāna Bhairava*. *See also* eight limbs of yoga.

DHARMA (*dharma*): Essential duty; the law of righteousness; living in accordance with the divine Will.

DHOTI(S) (*dhotī*): Traditional dress for men in India; a length of cloth wrapped around the waist.

DHYANA (*dhyāna*): Meditation; the seventh stage of *yoga* described by Patanjali in the *Yoga Sūtras*. *See also* eight limbs of yoga.

DINESHA (*dinesha*): (*lit.* lord of the day) The sun.

DIVINE NAME: A name of God. Silent repetition or chanting of the names of God fills the heart with devotion, love, and bliss, and is considered to be the most effective means of redemption in *Kaliyuga*, the present age.

Glossary

DURGA (*durgā*): (*lit.* hard to conquer) The fierce aspect of the universal Shakti or divine Mother, who destroys limitations and evil tendencies. She is often depicted as an eight-armed warrior goddess who rides a tiger and carries weapons.

DWARAKA (*dwaraka*): An ancient town on the west coast of India; the capital of Lord Krishna's kingdom. Dwaraka's shrine to Lord Krishna is considered one of the principal holy places of pilgrimage.

EIGHT GREAT SIDDHIS: *See* siddhis.

EIGHT LIMBS OF YOGA (*yoga*): The eight stages of *ashtānga* or *rāja yoga*, described by Patanjali in the *Yoga Sūtras* as: self-restraint — the *yamas* of non-violence, truthfulness, non-stealing, continence, and non-acquisitiveness; daily practices — the *niyamas* of purity, contentment, austerity, study of scriptures, and surrender to God; steady posture (*āsana*); breath control (*prānāyāma*); sense withdrawal (*pratyāhāra*); concentration (*dhārana*); meditation (*dhyāna*); and union with the Absolute (*samādhi*).

EKALAVYA (*ekalavya*): A tribal boy who wanted to learn archery from the great royal teacher, Dronacharya. When Drona rejected him as a disciple because he was of low caste, Ekalavya mastered the skills of archery and equalled Arjuna, the greatest archer of all, by meditating on a clay image of the Guru with deep devotion. He is cited as an example of ideal discipleship. His story is told in the *Mahābhārata*.

FIGURE ONE: In his writings, Swami Muktananda often describes the significance of the inner Self in relation to worldly attainments by using the analogy of the power of the figure one to turn a line of zeros into a number of great value, for example, a million. No matter how long the line of zeros, without the figure one, they will never amount to anything.

FIVE ELEMENTS: Earth, water, fire, air, and ether.

FIVE SHEATHS: The five coverings of an embodied soul, which determine personality and the nature of the individual consciousness. *Annamaya kosha,* composed of food, constitutes the gross body; *prānamaya kosha* corresponds roughly to the nervous system or vital being; *manomaya kosha* is the mind;

Glossary

vijñānamaya kosha is the intellect; *ānandamaya kosha* is the sheath of bliss.

FIVE-SYLLABLE MANTRA: *See* Namah Shivaya.

FOUR BODIES: The soul has four bodies—physical, subtle, causal, and supracausal—that are experienced, respectively, in the waking, dream, deep sleep, and *samādhi* states.

FOUR CASTES: *See* caste.

FOUR LIGHTS: Red, white, black, and blue light(s), experienced primarily in meditative states, are associated, respectively, with the physical, subtle, causal, and supracausal bodies of the soul.

FOUR VEDAS: *See* Vedas.

GANESHA (*ganesha*): The elephant-headed god, also known as Ganapati, who is especially popular in Maharashtra. The son of Lord Shiva and Goddess Parvati, he is worshiped at the beginning of any undertaking, as well as in many festivals, as the god of wisdom, the destroyer of sorrows, and the remover of obstacles.

GANESHPURI (*ganeshapurī*): A village at the foot of Mandagni Mountain in Maharashtra, India. Bhagawan Nityananda settled in this region where *yogis* have performed spiritual practices for thousands of years. The *ashram* founded by Swami Muktananda at his Guru's command, is built on this sacred land. *See also* Gurudev Siddha Peeth.

GANGA, GANGES (*gangā*): The most sacred river of India, the Ganges is said to descend from heaven through Lord Shiva's matted hair. On earth, it flows down from the Himalayas, across all of north India to the Bay of Bengal. It is believed that all sins are purified by a dip in its holy waters; each year, many devout Hindus make the pilgrimage to its source in the ice caves of Gangotri.

GAURI (*gaurī*): A name of Goddess Parvati, Lord Shiva's consort, meaning "white complexioned."

GHEE (*ghī*): Clarified butter used in Indian cooking and in worship.

GIRNAR (*girnar*): A sacred mountain in Gujarat, considered to be the abode of many holy and divine beings, including Lord Dattatreya (Guru Datta) and the Siddha, Gorakhnath.

Glossary

GITA, BHAGAVAD GITA (*bhagavad gītā*): (*lit.* Song of the Lord) One of the world's greatest works of spiritual literature, part of the epic *Mahābhārata*. In the *Gītā*, Lord Krishna explains the path of liberation to Arjuna on the battlefield, before the fighting begins. *See also* Mahabharata.

GODDESS OF KNOWLEDGE: *See* Saraswati

GOKUL (*gokul*): A town in north India where Lord Krishna spent his boyhood as the foster-child of Nanda, a cowherd.

GOLOKA (*goloka*): (*lit.* world of the cows) The most sacred part of *Vaikuntha*, Lord Vishnu's celestial abode; a symbol of purity and bliss.

GOPI CHAND (*gopī chand*): A king who had 700 wives.

GOVINDA (*govinda*): (*lit.* master of the cows) Lord of the senses and the mind. In the *Bhagavad Gītā*, an epithet of young Krishna.

GURU, GURUDEV (*guru, gurudeva*): (*lit. gu*, darkness; *ru*, light; *deva*, divine) A spiritual Master who has attained oneness with God and who is therefore able both to initiate seekers and to guide them on the spiritual path to liberation. A Guru is also required to be learned in the scriptures and must belong to a lineage of Masters. *See also* shaktipat; Siddha.

GURUBHAKTA (*gurubhakta*): A devotee of the Guru.

GURUBHAVA (*gurubhāva*): (bhava *lit.* becoming, being) A feeling of absorption or identification with the Guru.

GURU DATTA, DATTATREYA (*guru datta, dattatreya*): A divine incarnation known as the lord of *avadhūtas* (enlightened beings who live in a state beyond body-consciousness); often revered as an embodiment of the supreme Guru.

GURUDEV SIDDHA PEETH (*pītha*): (Siddha Peeth, *lit.* abode of the perfected beings) The main ashram of Siddha Yoga and the site of the Samadhi shrine of Swami Muktananda. It was founded in 1956 when Bhagawan Nityananda instructed Swami Muktananda to live in a simple three-room compound near Ganeshpuri, India. Charged with the power of divine Consciousness, the ashram is a world-renowned center for spiritual practice and study under the guidance of the living Master, Swami Chidvilasananda. *See also* ashram; Ganeshpuri.

Glossary

GURUKRIPA (*gurukripā*): (*lit.* Guru's grace) The divine energy bestowed on a seeker through the compassion of the Guru. *See also* shaktipat.

GURUKULA (*gurukula*): (*lit.* school of the Master) In ancient times, students served the Guru at his house or *ashram* for 8, 12, 24, or 36 years before receiving sacred initiation or *dīksha*. During this period, they observed celibacy (*brahmacharya*), studied the scriptures, and practiced self-inquiry and other spiritual disciplines in a tranquil forested environment under the guidance of the Master.

GURUMAYI (*gurumayī*): (*lit.* one who is absorbed in the Guru) A term of respect and endearment often used in addressing Swami Chidvilasananda.

GURUMUDRA (*gurumudrā*): *See* mudra; Shambhavi mudra.

GURU'S NAME: The *mantra* that has been received from the Guru and that is vibrant with his spiritual power of grace is considered to be the Guru's true "name." *See also* mantra.

GURUPRASAD (*guruprasāda*): A gift that carries the Guru's power of blessing; may refer to an external object, but often signifies an inner gift of grace. *See also* prasad.

HAM (*ham*): *See* ajapa-japa; So'ham-Hamsa.

HAMSA (*hamsa*): (*lit.* I am That) *See* So'ham-Hamsa.

HARA (*hara*): A name of Lord Shiva meaning "redeemer." *See also* Shiva.

HARI, HARI-GURU (*hari*): An epithet that is applied to the Master, implying that the Guru is like Lord Vishnu, an aspect of the supreme Lord, "the one who stills the fluctuations of the mind." *See also* Vishnu.

HATHA YOGA (*hatha yoga*): A yogic discipline in which various bodily and mental exercises are practiced for the purpose of awakening the *kundalinī shakti*. The awakened Shakti purifies the 72 million *nādīs*, resulting in an even flow of the incoming and outgoing breaths (*prāna* and *apāna*), and the experience of stillness of mind, or *samādhi*.

HEART LOTUS: The 12-petaled subtle energy center of the heart. *See* chakra.

Glossary

INDRA (*indra*): The lord of heaven and king of the gods; the god of thunder, lightning, and rain.

INNER SENSE PERCEPTION: The perception of inner lights, sounds, smells, tastes, and feelings in meditation. *See also* Kundalini; shaktipat.

JANARDANA (*janārdana*): A name of Lord Krishna meaning "one who makes demons tremble."

JAPA (*japa*): (*lit.* prayer uttered in a low voice) Repetition of a *mantra*; either silently or aloud. *See also* mantra.

JIVA (*jīva*): (*lit.* living being) The individual soul, as it appears conditioned by the experiences and the limitations of the body and the mind.

JIVANMUKTA (*jīvanmukta*): One who is liberated while still living in a physical body.

JNANA (YOGA) (*jñāna*): The *yoga* of knowledge; a spiritual path based on continuous contemplation and self-inquiry.

JNANESHA (*jñānesha*): (*lit.* lord of knowledge) The god of wisdom.

JNANI(S) (*jñāni*): An enlightened being; a follower of the path of knowledge. *See* jnana yoga.

KABIR (*kabīr*): (1440-1518) A great poet-saint, also known as Kabir Sahib or Kabirdas, who worked as a weaver in Benares. His followers included both Hindus and Muslims, and his influence was a strong force in overcoming the fierce religious factionalism of the day.

KAILAS (*kailāsa*): A mountain peak in the Tibetan region of the Himalayas, revered as the abode of Lord Shiva and a sacred place of pilgrimage.

KALI (*kālī*): (*lit.* the black one) The fearsome aspect of the universal Mother, or Shakti; Kali embodies the consuming power of time.

KALIYUGA (*kaliyuga*): (*lit.* the dark age) The present age, or world cycle, described as the Iron Age, in which righteousness and truth have degenerated; the age of moral and spiritual decadence, at the end of which the world will be purified.

KAPILA (*kapila*): A sacred river that runs through Karnataka State.

KARMA (*karma*): (*lit.* action) 1) Any action—physical, verbal, or

Glossary

mental; 2) destiny, which is caused by past actions, mainly those of previous lives.

KARMA YOGA: The yoga of action. A spiritual path expounded by Lord Krishna in the *Bhagavad Gītā* in which one performs actions as an offering to God, while remaining detached from the fruits of those actions.

KASHI (*kāshī*): The city of Varanasi, or Benares, sacred to Lord Shiva, located in north India on the banks of the river Ganges. According to Hindu tradition, whoever dies in this city attains liberation.

KASHMIR SHAIVISM: A non-dual philosophy that recognizes the entire universe as a manifestation of one divine conscious energy; a branch of the Shaivite philosophical tradition that explains how the formless supreme Principle, Shiva, manifests as the universe. Together with Vedanta, Kashmir Shaivism provides the basic scriptural context for Siddha Yoga Meditation.

KAVERI (*kāverī*): A sacred river that flows through the states of Karnataka and Tamil Nadu in south India.

KEDAR (*kedārnath*): A sacred center in the Himalayas, close to the Tibetan border between Badrinath and the source of the river Ganges at Gangotri.

KESHAVA (*keshava*): A name of Lord Krishna meaning "slayer of the demon Keshi." The story is told in the *Srīmad Bhāgavatam*.

KHECHARI (*khecharī avasthā*): The state in which one roams in the inner spiritual sky; the bliss of movement in the vast expanse of Consciousness.

KECHARI MUDRA (*khecharī mudrā*): An advanced yogic pose in which the tongue is thrust up. This *mudrā* pierces the *rudra granthi* (knot of Rudra) in the *sushumnā nādī*, causing the meditator to experience *samādhi* and taste divine nectar. *See also* three knots.

KING OF THE MOUNTAINS: *See* Uplifter of the mountain.

KRISHNA (*krishna*): (*lit.* the dark one; the one who attracts irresistibly) The eighth incarnation of Lord Vishnu. His life story is told in the *Srīmad Bhāgavatam*; His spiritual teachings are contained in the *Bhagavad Gītā*, a portion of the epic *Mahābhārata*. *See also* Vishnu.

Glossary

KRIYA(S) (*krīyā*): (*lit.* movement(s)) Physical, mental, or emotional movement initiated by the awakened *kundalinī;* purificatory movements.

KUMBHAKA (*kumbhaka*): Voluntary or involuntary retention of the breath; a process of *prāṇāyāma,* or breath control, described in *rāja yoga* and *hatha yoga. Kumbhaka* occurs when the inward and outward flow of *prāṇa* becomes stabilized.

KUNDALINI (*kundalinī*): (*lit.* coiled one) The supreme power, primordial Shakti, or energy that lies coiled at the base of the spine in the *mūlādhāra chakra* of every human being. Through the descent of grace (*shaktipāt*), this extremely subtle force, also described as a goddess, is awakened and begins to purify the whole system. As She travels upward through the central channel (*sushumnā nāḍī*), She pierces the various subtle energy centers (*chakras*) until She finally reaches the *sahasrāra* at the crown of the head. There, the individual self merges into the supreme Self in the marriage of Shiva and Shakti, and the cycle of birth and death comes to an end. Kundalini is described, in the sacred texts that praise Her, as constantly watching for an opportunity to bestow Her grace on the seeker. *See also* chakra, shaktipat.

LAKSHMI (*lakshmī*): An aspect of the divine Mother; the beautiful goddess of prosperity and abundance; portrayed as the consort of Lord Vishnu, the sustainer of the universe, She is the source of all material and spiritual blessings and auspiciousness.

LALLI YOGINI, LALLESHWARI (*lallī yoginī*): A great *yoginī* of Kashmir whose devotional poems were often quoted by Swami Muktananda; his rendering of her poetry is published in Hindi and English under the title *Lalleshwari.*

LAYA YOGA (*laya yoga*): Absorption of the mind into the Self; the interiorization of consciousness.

LIMBS OF YOGA: *See* eight limbs of yoga.

LINGA (*linga*): *See* shivalinga.

LOKA (*loka*): (lit. world) A world or plane of existence.

MADALASA (*madālasā*): A queen of ancient India and the daughter of a sage. She determined the destiny of her seven sons by the manner in which she raised them. The first six, hearing

Glossary

constantly about the Self, became sages; the last, taught to be strong and courageous, became a king.

MAHA (*mahā*): Great, mighty, powerful, lofty, noble.

MAHABHARATA (*mahābhārata*): An epic poem in Sanskrit, composed by the sage Vyasa, which recounts the struggle between the Kaurava and Pandava brothers over the disputed kingdom of Bharat. Within this vast narrative is contained a wealth of Indian secular and religious lore. The *Bhagavad Gītā* occurs in the latter portion of the *Mahābhārata*.

MAHADEVA (*mahādeva*): (*lit.* great god) One of the names of Lord Shiva.

MAHALOKA (*mahāloka*): (*lit.* great world) The vast world of inner experience; in his spiritual autobiography, *Play of Consciousness*, Swami Muktananda describes his visions of the inner worlds that culminated in the experience of the entire universe emanating from and contained within the Blue Pearl in the *sahasrāra*, the highest center of consciousness.

MAHAMUDRA (*mahāmudrā*): (*lit.* great seal) *See* mudra; Shambhavi mudra.

MAHAPRASAD (*mahāprasāda*): (*lit.* great gift that carries blessings) Guru's grace; the awakening of the divine inner energy in a seeker. *See also* shaktipat.

MAHARISHI(S) (*mahārishi*): (*lit.* great seer) A great sage. It was to the *rishis* that the sacred mantras and the knowledge of the Vedas were revealed during high meditative states.

MAHASHAKTI (*mahāshakti*): (*lit.* great cosmic energy) A name of the Goddess. *See also* Chiti; Shakti.

MAHAYAJNA (*mahāyajña*): (*lit.* great sacrifice, great offering) *See* yajna.

MAITREYI (*maitreyī*): The young wife of the sage Yajnavalkya, who appears in the *Brihadāranyaka Upanishad*. She was a seeker who renounced her husband's worldly wealth and sought instead his spiritual wisdom.

MALA (*māla*): A string of beads, used like a rosary to facilitate a state of concentration on the *mantra*. *See also* japa.

MANDODARI (*mandodarī*): The chaste wife of Ravana, the demon

Glossary

king who kidnapped the wife of Lord Rama. Her story is told in the *Rāmāyana*.

MANTRA (*mantra*): (*lit.* sacred invocation; that which protects) The names of God; sacred words or divine sounds invested with the power to protect, purify, and transform the individual who repeats them.

MANTRA YOGA (*mantra yoga*): The *yoga* of the divine Word; the science of sound. The path to union through *mantra yoga* is based on repetition of the name(s) of God and contemplation of their meaning. *See also* mantra deity; mantraprasad.

MANTRA-DEITY: The deity named by or identified with the *mantra*, to whom its repetition is offered as worship.

MANTRAPRASAD (*mantraprasāda*): (*lit.* gift of the mantra) A *mantra* is alive, full of consciousness (*chaitanya*), only when it is received as a gift from the enlightened Guru who has repeated it and realized its power. The Guru enters the disciple in the form of the *mantra. See also* shaktipat.

MANU (*manu*): The first man; the father of the human race; the lawgiver of Indian tradition.

MATHURA (*mathurā*): A sacred town in north India where Lord Krishna was born to Devaki in a prison cell.

MAULAWI (*maulawī*): A Muslim religious scholar.

MAYA (*māyā*): The power of illusion; the indefinable power of the supreme Being that projects the illusion of the universe; ensnaring power.

MENTAL WORSHIP: Worship of a deity that is performed or visualized entirely in the mind or imagination.

MOKSHA (*moksha*): The state of liberation; enlightenment; freedom.

MUDRA (*mudrā*): (*lit.* seal) A symbolic gesture or movement of the hand expressive of an inner state, such as joy, fearlessness, liberation. Deities and saints are often pictured performing these gestures to bestow their blessings. Also, advanced *hatha yoga* techniques practiced to hold the *prāna* (life force) within the body, forcing the *kundalinī* to flow into the *sushumnā*. *Mudrās* can occur spontaneously after receiving *shaktipāt*.

MUKTABAI: A 13th century woman saint of India; the sister of

Glossary

Jnaneshwar Maharaj, the greatest *yogi* and poet-saint of Maharashtra. She and her three brothers were enlightened at a very early age.

MULADHARA (*mūlādhāra*): The first *chakra*, or lowest of the seven major energy centers in the subtle body, situated at the base of the spine, where consciousness deals mainly with survival. Here the *kundalinī shakti* lies coiled three-and-a-half times, sleeping, dormant until awakened by grace. *See also* chakra; Kundalini; shaktipat.

NADA (*nāda*): (*lit.* sound) Inner sounds heard during advanced stages of meditation; celestial harmonies; the spontaneous unstruck sound experienced in the *sushumnā nādī*.

NADI(S) (*nādī*): (*lit.* duct, nerve) A channel in the subtle body through which the vital force flows. A network of 72 million *nādīs* spreads throughout the human body. The three main *nādīs* are the central channel, or *sushumnā*, which is flanked by the *idā* and *pingalā nādīs*, known as the channels of the moon and the sun. The hubs or junction points of the *nādīs* are known as *chakras*. *See also* chakra; Kundalini.

NAMAH SHIVAYA (*namah shivāya*): A five-syllable Sanskrit *mantra*, meaning "I bow to Shiva, the supreme Self." *See also* Om Namah Shivaya.

NAME, THE: A name of God. Silent repetition or audible chanting of divine Names is considered to be the most effective means of redemption in *Kaliyuga*, the present age. Chanting and *japa* open the heart to the love and joy contained within it.

NARA (*nara*): A human being.

NARAYANA (*nārāyana*): A name of Lord Vishnu meaning "the sole refuge of all creatures."

NARAYANI (*nārāyanī*): A name of Lakshmi, meaning the consort, or feminine power, of Lord Vishnu. *See also* Lakshmi.

NARMADA (*narmadā*): A sacred river that flows through the states of Madhya Pradesh and Maharashtra in India.

NEELA, NEELESHWARI (*nīla, nīleshwarī*): (*lit.* Blue Goddess) *See* Blue Pearl.

NINE RIDDHIS: *See* riddhis.

Glossary

NINETEEN SUBTLE MOUTHS: These are speech, grasping, locomotion, procreation, and excretion (the five organs of action); hearing, seeing, touching, tasting, and smelling (the five organs of perception); the five vital airs or *pranas*; and the conscious mind, intellect, ego, and unconscious mind (the four psychic instruments).

NIRVIKALPA SAMADHI (*nirvikalpa samādhi*): (*lit. samādhi* without form) The highest state of meditative union with the Absolute that is beyond attribute, thought, or image.

NITYANANDA, BHAGAWAN (*nityānanda bhagawān*): (d.1961; *lit.* the lord of eternal bliss) Also known as Bade Baba (Big Baba). Very little is known of Bhagawan Nityananda's early life; it seems he was a born Siddha, living his entire life in the highest state of consciousness. He was seen first in South India and later traveled to Maharashtra, where the village of Ganeshpuri grew up around him. He spoke very little, yet thousands of people would queue for hours for a glimpse of him and to experience the profound blessing of his presence. His Samadhi shrine is located at the site of his original quarters in Ganeshpuri, about a mile from Gurudev Siddha Peeth, the principal ashram of Siddha Yoga Meditation. In both Gurudev Siddha Peeth and Shree Muktananda Ashram in South Fallsburg, New York, Swami Muktananda has dedicated a temple of meditation to honor Bhagawan Nityananda's *murti*, or statue.

OM: The primal sound from which the universe emanates. Also written *Aum*, it is the inner essence of all mantras.

OM NAMAH SHIVAYA (*om namah shivāya*): (*lit.* Om, I bow to Shiva) The Sanskrit mantra of the Siddha lineage is known as the great redeeming mantra because of its power to grant both worldly fulfillment and spiritual realization. *Om* is the primordial sound; *Shiva* denotes divine Consciousness, the Lord who dwells in every heart.

PADMABHUSHAN (*padmabhūshan*): The third highest title of honor awarded by the National Government of India for achievements in the Arts and Humanities.

PAISE (*paise*): The smallest Indian coin. One hundred *paise* make a *rupee*.

PANDIT (*pandit*): A Hindu religious scholar; a priest.

Glossary

PARABRAHMAN (*parabrahman*): The supreme Absolute, whose nature is described in Vedantic philosophy as Existence, Consciousness, and Bliss.

PARASHIVA (*parāshiva*): (*lit.* supreme Shiva) The highest *tattva* or principle of creation as described in the non-dual philosophy of Kashmir Shaivism; the Lord; the supreme Guru; the source of the grace-bestowing power of the Guru.

PARASHIVA-SHAKTI-MUDRA (*parāshivashaktimudrā*): The transcendental state in which the absolute unity of Shiva and Shakti is experienced. *See also* Kundalini; Shakti; Shiva.

PARVATI (*parvati*): (*lit.* daughter of the mountains) The wife of Lord Shiva and the daughter of the King of the Himalayas; a name of the universal Mother or Shakti.

PRANA (*prāna*): The vital life-sustaining force of both the body and the universe. To carry out its work, *prāna* pervades the body in five forms: *prāna*, inhalation, the primary support of the heart; *apāna*, exhalation, the power that works downward to expel waste matter; *samāna*, the power that distributes the nourishment from food to all parts of the body; *vyāna*, the power of movement within the 72 million *nādīs*, or nerve channels of the subtle body; and *udāna*, the power that carries energy upward, giving strength and radiance to the body.

PRANA-APANA (*prāna-apāna*): The respiratory process of inhalation and exhalation. *See also* ajapa-japa; So'ham-Hamsa.

PRASAD (*prasāda*): A blessed or divine gift; often refers to food that has first been offered to God and later distributed.

PREMA (*prema*): Divine love. *See also* bhakti.

PUJA(S) (*pūjā*): Worship. 1) The performance of worship. 2) An altar with images of the Guru or deity and objects used in worship.

PUSHKAR (*pushkāra*): A center of pilgrimage in Rajasthan, India, that is sacred to Brahma, the Creator.

RADHE SHYAM (*rādhe shyām*): A name of Lord Krishna meaning the dark-blue complexioned beloved of Radha. She was the chief of the *gopīs*, the milkmaids of Vrindavan, who were the childhood companions of young Krishna. Radha is celebrated as the embodiment of devotion.

Glossary

RAJA YOGA (*rāja yoga*): The discipline of quieting the mind according to Patanjali's *Yoga Sūtras*; it includes concentration, meditation, and *samādhi*. *See also* eight limbs of yoga.

RAMA (*rāma*): The seventh incarnation of Lord Vishnu, Rama is seen as the embodiment of *dharma* and is the object of great devotion. He is the central character in the Indian epic *Rāmāyana*. *See also* Ramayana.

RAMAYANA (*rāmāyana*): Attributed to the sage Valmiki, and one of the great epic poems of India, the *Rāmāyana* recounts the life and exploits of Lord Rama, the seventh incarnation of Vishnu. Rama, son of the King of Ayodhya, is forced into exile in the forest with his wife, Sita (a form of Lakshmi), and his brother, Lakshmana. Later, Sita is captured by the demon king Ravana and taken to Sri Lanka. She is rescued by Rama, with the help of Hanuman, chief of the monkeys and an embodiment of devotion and service to the Lord. The story, rich with characters, sub-plots, and spiritual meaning, has been told and retold through the ages by saints, poets, scholars, and common folk.

RAMESHWAR, RAMESHWARAM (*rāmeshwaram*): A sacred place in Tamil Nadu, South India. Here, Lord Rama set up a *Shivalinga* (an oval-shaped emblem of Lord Shiva) and worshiped it to achieve victory over the demon Ravana, whose kingdom was just across the bay in Sri Lanka. *See also* Ramayana.

RED AURA: *See* Four Lights.

RIDDHI(S) (*riddhi*): The lesser powers, such as wealth, fame, and success. *See also* siddhis.

RISHI (*rishi*): A seer of truth.

RISHIKESH (*rīshikesha*): A sacred place on the banks of the Ganges, high in the Himalayas where the ancient sages (*rishis*) gathered.

RUPEE (*rūpee*): A small unit of Indian currency.

SADASHIVA (*sadāshiva*): The all-pervading Lord Shiva. *See also* Shiva.

SADGURU (*sadguru*): A true Guru; divine Master. *See also* Guru.

SADHAKA (*sādhaka*): A seeker on the spiritual path. *See also* sadhana.

Glossary

SADHANA (*sādhana*): A spiritual discipline or path; practices, both physical and mental, on the spiritual path.

SADHU (*sādhu*): A wandering monk or ascetic; a holy being; a practitioner of *sādhana*.

SAH (*sah*): *See* So'ham-Hamsa.

SAHAJA-JAPA (*sahaja-japa*): (*lit.* natural repetition of the mantra) *See* So'ham-Hamsa.

SAHASRANAMA (*sahasranāma*): (*lit.* thousand names) There are many *sahasranāmas*. Swami Muktananda refers to the *Vishnu Sahasranāma*, a hymn celebrating Lord Vishnu that is sung regularly in Siddha Yoga Meditation ashrams. *See also* Vishnu.

SAHASRARA (*sahasrāra*): The thousand-petaled *chakra*, or spiritual energy center, at the crown of the head, where one experiences the highest states of consciousness. It is the seat of Lord Shiva, the supreme Guru. When the *kundalinī shakti* unites with Shiva in the *sahasrāra*, the meditator achieves the state of enlightenment, or Self-realization. *See also* chakra; Kundalini.

SAMADHI (*samādhi*): The state of meditative union with the Absolute. *See also* eight limbs of yoga.

SAMADHI SHRINE: After their *māhāsamādhi* (*lit.* the great *samādhi* or final union of the individual consciousness with the Absolute), great *yogīs* and saints are buried seated in a yogic posture and surrounded with precious and sacred objects. Being pervaded by the rays of their divine love and wisdom, the saints' resting places are tended with the utmost reverence as centers of prayer and meditation, and a source of blessings for all who come there.

SAMSARA (*samsāra*): The world of change, mutability, and death; the world of becoming.

SAMYAMA (*samyama*): The threefold technique of *yoga*, comprising *dhārana, dhyāna,* and *samādhi,* by means of which the innermost nature of anything can be directly perceived, or the direct knowledge of the universe gained. *See also* eight limbs of yoga.

SANNYASA (*sannyāsa*): Monkhood; the ceremony and vows in which one renounces the responsibilities and privileges of worldly life and dedicates oneself exclusively to the goal of Self-realization and service; the fourth and final stage of life in the Hindu tradition.

SANNYASI(N) (*sannyāsī*): One who has become a monk by taking formal vows of renunciation; wearer of the ochre robe.

SARASWATI (*saraswatī*): (*lit.* the flowing one) 1) A sacred river that flows from Haryana through the Punjab and Rajasthan. 2) An aspect of the divine Mother; the Shakti, or creative power of the Lord; the goddess of speech, learning, and the arts, who has taken the form of the Sanskrit alphabet and who is worshiped by students, teachers, scholars, artists, and musicians; the Muse. Dressed in white and riding a peacock that symbolizes the unfolding of the creative power, with two of her hands She plays a *vīna*; in Her other two hands She holds a book and a *japa māla*.

SARI(S) (*sārī*): Indian dress for women that covers the entire body; an emblem of modesty.

SARVAJNALOKA (*sarvajñaloka*): (*lit.* world of omniscience) The state or subtle center of omniscience.

SATCHIDANANDA (*saccidānanda*): (*lit.* absolute Existence, Consciousness, and Bliss) The three indivisible categories used in Vedantic philosophy to describe the experience of the Absolute.

SATSANG (*satsanga*): (*lit.* the company of the truth) The company of saints and devotees; a gathering of devotees for the purpose of chanting, meditating, and listening to scriptural teachings or readings.

SATTVIC (*sattva*): Pure; full of the quality of light. *See also* three gunas.

SAVITRI (*sāvitrī*): The supremely loyal wife who saved her husband Satyavan from the clutches of death and brought him to glory and prosperity; a symbol of wifely chastity and fidelity. Her story appears in the *Mahābhārata*.

SEASON-ABIDING: *See* brahmacharis.

SEED LETTERS (*bīja mantra*): Basic sounds from the Sanskrit language, the repetition of which manifests the object, deity, or state that they represent. Each chakra contains seed letters or syllables that embody its power and consciousness.

Glossary

SELF: *See* Atman.

SELF-REALIZATION: The state of enlightenment in which the individual merges with pure Consciousness. *See also* Siddha.

SEVA (*sevā*): (*lit.* service) Selfless service; work offered to God, performed with an attitude of nondoership and without attachment.

SHAIVA(S), SHAIVITE: The devotees of Lord Shiva. *See also* Kashmir Shaivism; Shiva.

SHAKTA(S) (*shākta*): The worshipers of Shakti. *See also* Chiti; Shakti.

SHAKTI (*shakti*): Force, energy; spiritual power; according to Shaivite philosophy, the divine or cosmic energy that manifests the universe; the dynamic aspect of supreme Shiva. *See also* Chiti; Kundalini.

SHAKTIPAT (*shaktipāt*): (*lit.* the descent of grace) The transmission of spiritual power, or Shakti, from the Guru to the disciple; spiritual awakening by grace.

SHALIGRAM (*shāligrām*): A naturally-formed round stone, found on the banks of the Gandaki river and worshiped as a symbol of Lord Vishnu.

SHAMBHAVI MUDRA (*shāmbhavī mudrā*): (*lit.* state of supreme Shiva) A state of spontaneous or effortless *samādhi* in which the eyes become focused within their own orbs, not seeing any outer objects. Breathing is suspended without any effort and the mind delights in the inner Self without any attempt at concentration. It is the usual *mudrā* of a Siddha.

SHIVA (*shiva*): A name for the all-pervasive supreme Reality. As the deity and highest Principle of the Shaivite tradition, He performs the five cosmic functions of creation, dissolution, maintenance, concealment, and grace-bestowal. He is 'sky-clad' because He is so pure. Also one of the Hindu trinity of gods, representing God as the destroyer; in His personal form, He is portrayed as a *yogī* wearing a tiger skin and holding a trident. Snakes coil around His neck and arms, and He is attended by a host of terrible goblins, ghosts, and demons. Paradoxically, He is also *karunābde*, "the ocean of compassion," and *ashutosha*, "He who is easily pleased." He is also portrayed in sweet family portraits with His spouse, Parvati, and their son, Ganesh. His dialogues with Parvati, in which He is the supreme Guru and She takes the part of the disciple to ask for knowledge of liberation, give rise to such sacred texts as *Srī Guru Gītā*, recited daily in Siddha Yoga Meditation ashrams.

SHIVALINGA (*shivalinga*): (lingam *lit.* mark or characteristic) Shiva's sacred symbol representing His creative power; an oval-shaped emblem of Lord Shiva, made of stone, metal, or clay.

SHIVARATRI (*shivarātrī*): (*lit.* night of Shiva) The night of the new moon in late February that is especially sacred to Lord Shiva. Devotees repeat the mantra *Om Namah Shivāya* throughout the night; on this night each repetition is said to equal the merit of a thousand repetitions.

SHIVO'HAM (*shivo'ham*): A mantra meaning "I am Shiva."

SHUKAMUNI (*shukamūni*): The son of Vyasa; very beautiful, absolutely pure, and all-knowing, he was considered the greatest saint of ancient India. He revealed the mysteries of the universe and the various spiritual paths to other seers during his boyhood, and is the narrator of the exploits of Lord Krishna to King Parikshit in the *Srīmad Bhāgavatam*.

SHYAM (*shyām*): (*lit.* dark blue) A name of Lord Krishna, who had a dark blue complexion. *See also* Radhe Shyam.

SIDDHA(S) (*siddha*): A perfected yogi; one who lives in the state of unity-consciousness and who has achieved mastery over the senses and their objects; one whose experience of the supreme Self is uninterrupted and whose identification with the ego has been dissolved.

SIDDHALOKA (*siddhaloka*): (*lit.* world of the perfected beings) A world of blue light, in which the great Siddha Masters dwell in perpetual bliss; described by Swami Muktananda in his spiritual autobiography *Play of Consciousness*.

SIDDHA MAHAYOGA (*mahāyoga*): (*lit.* the great yoga) A path to union of the individual and the Divine that begins with *shaktipāt*, the inner awakening by the grace of a Siddha Guru. Swami Chidvilasananda, Swami Muktananda's chosen successor, is the living Master of this path. Siddha Yoga is known as *mahāyoga*, because *shaktipāt* initiation sets in motion a

Glossary

spontaneous and intelligent process in which all or any form of *yoga* will occur within the seeker according to need and temperament. *See also* Guru; Kundalini; shaktipat.

SIDDHI(S) (*siddhi*): Occult or supernatural powers attained through yogic practices. The eight major *siddhis* are *anima,* the power of becoming as small as an atom; *mahima,* the power to expand to any size; *laghima,* the power to levitate, to become light; *garima,* the power to become heavy; *prapti,* the power to attain everything; *prakamya,* the power of seeing one's wishes fulfilled; *ishatva,* the power of lordship over everything; *vashitva,* the power to attract and control.

SINDHU (*sindhu*): A sacred river in north India.

SITA (*sītā*): (*lit.* daughter of the earth) An embodiment of Lakshmi and the wife of Lord Rama, the seventh incarnation of Lord Vishnu. Their story is told in the epic *Rāmāyana.*

SIX LOTUSES: *See* chakra.

SIX CHAKRAS: *See* chakra.

SIX PURIFICATORY EXERCISES: Exercises practiced by *hatha yogis* to cleanse the body. They are *neti* (nasal wash), *dhauti* (stomach wash), *kapalabhati* (cleaning the sinuses), *trataka* (cleaning the eyes), *nauli* (cleaning the abdominal organs), and *basti* (cleaning the large colon).

SIX SCHOOLS OF PHILOSOPHY: The six branches of ancient Indian philosophy are: Sankhya, Yoga, Nyaya, Vaisheshika, Purva Mimamsa, and Uttara Mimamsa, also known as Vedanta.

SKY-BLUE LIGHT: *See* Blue Pearl.

SKY-BLUE RIVER: *See* Blue Pearl.

SO'HAM-HAMSA (*so'ham-hamsa*): (*lit.* I am That) *So'ham* and *Hamsa* are identical *mantras* that describe the natural vibration of the Self, which occurs spontaneously with each incoming and outgoing breath. The breath is drawn in with the sound *sah,* and goes out with the sound *aham.* This process is described in detail by Swami Muktananda in his book *I Am That.* By becoming aware of *Hamsa,* a seeker experiences the identity between the individual self and the supreme Self.

Glossary

SON OF NANDA (*nanda*): A name of Lord Krishna that honors Nanda, his foster father.

SRI (*srī*): Sri Guru, Sri Rama, Sri Vishnu, etc. A term of respect that means "wealth, prosperity, glory, and success," and signifies mastery of all these.

SRIMAD BHAGAVATAM (*srīmad bhāgavatam*): One of the Puranas, it consists of ancient legends of the various incarnations of the Lord, including the life and exploits of Lord Krishna, and stories of the sages and their disciples.

SRIRANGA, SRIRANGAM (*srīrangam*): A famous south Indian temple, where Lord Vishnu is worshiped.

SUBTLE BODY: *See* Four bodies.

SURYA(S) (*sūrya*): Worshipers of Surya, the sun god.

SUSHUMNA (*sushumnā*): The central and most important of all the 72 million subtle nerve channels in the human body, the *sushumnā* extends from the *mūlādhāra chakra* at the base of the spine to the *sahasrāra*, or crown chakra, and contains all the other *chakras*, or subtle energy centers. When the *prāna*, or vital force, constantly flows through it, one becomes enlightened. *See also* chakra.

SWADHYAYA (*swādhyāya*): The study of the Self; the regular disciplined practice of chanting and recitation of spiritual texts.

TA THAI! TA THAI!: Syllables indicating rhythm for percussion instruments and dances.

TANDRALOKA (*tandraloka*): (*lit.* world of tandra) The state or center of higher consciousness between sleeping and waking that is experienced in meditation.

TANTRAS (*tantras*): *See* yoga tantras.

TAPA, TAPAS (*tapas*): (*lit.* heat) Austerities; also the experience of heat called "the fire of yoga." Generated during the practice and process of *yoga* (by the friction between the mind and the heart and between the demands of the senses and the impulse toward renunciation), this fire burns away the impurities that stand between a seeker and the truth.

TAPASYA: *See* tapa.

TARA (*tārā*): The chaste wife of Bali, the monkey-king. Her story is told in the *Rāmāyana*.

Glossary

THAT: When capitalized, it refers to the inner Self or to the supreme Absolute. *See* Atman.

THREE IMPURITIES: The three *malas* (taints or limitations) assumed by the supreme Being in order to manifest Himself. By *anava mala*, the universal becomes individual; by *maya mala*, the undifferentiated becomes differentiated; by *karma mala*, the non-doer becomes the doer.

THREE GUNAS (*gūnas*): The three primal qualities that form the nature of things: *sattva*, the quality that illumines, clarity; *rajas*, the quality that drives one to action, passion; *tamas*, the quality that hides or darkens, inertia.

THREE KNOTS (*granthi*): The three junction points in the *sushumnā* (central channel) where the *idā, pingalā,* and *sushumnā nādīs* converge and form a knot. *Brahma granthi* is located in the *mūlādhāra chakra, Vishnu granthi* is located in the heart *chakra*, and *Rudra granthi* is located in the *ājñā chakra*. These knots bind the individual into false identification with the gross, subtle, and causal bodies. When *kundalinī* is awakened and rises up through the *sushumnā*, She pierces these knots as She ascends to the *sahasrāra*. *See also* chakra; nadi.

THREE STATES: The waking, dream, and deep sleep states.

THREEFOLD SAMYAMA: *See* samyama.

THROBBING OF CONSCIOUSNESS (*spanda*): The vibration of divine Consciousness that pervades all life and is perceived by the yogi in higher states of meditation.

THUMB-SIZED FLAME: *See* four lights.

TRIKUTI (*trikutī*): The junction at the *ājñā chakra*, in the forehead between the eyebrows, where the three main *nādīs*, (subtle nerve channels), *idā, pingalā,* and *sushumnā*, converge. *See also* chakra; nadi.

TULSI (*tulasī*): An Indian herb similar to basil that is used in the worship of Lord Vishnu. It has great medicinal virtues.

TURIYA (*turīya*): The fourth or transcendental state, beyond the waking, dream, and deep sleep states, in which the true nature of reality is directly perceived; the state of *samādhi* or deep meditation. *See also* four bodies.

Glossary

UMA (*umā*): A name of the divine Mother or Shakti, Lord Shiva's consort, meaning "don't be sad" and "ever-young"; the power of divine Will.

UNIVERSAL MOTHER: *See* Chiti; Shakti.

UPANISHADS (*upanishads*): (*lit.* sitting near steadfastly) The inspired teachings, visions, and mystical experiences of the ancient sages, or *rishis*, of India. These scriptures, exceeding 100 texts, constitute "the end" or "final understanding" *anta* of the Vedas; hence the term *Vedānta*. With immense variety of form and style, all of these texts give the same essential teaching, that the individual soul and God (Brahman) are one. *See also* Vedanta.

UPLIFTER OF THE MOUNTAIN; KING OF THE MOUNTAINS: Lord Krishna protected His people from tempestuous rains by lifting up a mountain on His little finger; Lord Shiva, who dwells in the Himalayas, is the King of the mountains. In verse 491 the gods Krishna and Shiva are seen as one.

VAIKUNTHA (*vaikuntha*): The celestial abode of Lord Vishnu.

VAIRAGI(S) (*vairāgī*): A sect of renunciants who worship Lord Rama.

VAISHNAVA(S) (*vaishnava*): Worshipers of Lord Vishnu.

VASISHTHA (*vāsishtha*): *See* Yoga Vasishtha.

VASUDEVA (*vāsudeva*): (*lit.* the luminous lord who dwells in all creatures as the inner Self) A name of Lord Krishna.

VEDANTA (*advaita vedānta*): (*lit.* the end of the Vedas) One of the six orthodox schools of Indian philosophy; the philosophy of absolute nondualism. *See also* Upanishads; Vedas.

VEDANTIN(S): Followers of Vedanta.

VEDAS (*vedas*): (*lit.* knowledge) Among the most ancient, sacred, and revered of the world's scriptures, the four Vedas are regarded as divinely revealed eternal wisdom. They are the *Rig Veda, Yajur Veda, Sāma Veda,* and *Atharva Veda.*

VEENA (*vīnā*): An Indian stringed musical instrument.

VIRYA (*vīrya*): The vital power of living creatures; seminal fluid.

VISHNU (*vishnu*): The all-pervasive supreme Reality; one of the

Glossary

Hindu trinity of gods, representing God as the sustainer of the universe; the deity of the Vaishnavas. In His personal form, He is portrayed as four-armed, holding a conch, a discus, a lotus, and a mace. He is dark blue in color. Vishnu incarnates in each *yuga* (cycle or world period) to protect and save the world when the knowledge of *dharma* (truth and righteousness) is lost. Rama and Krishna are the best known of His incarnations (*avatāras*).

VOID: The state in which there is no consciousness of knower, knowledge, or that which is known.

VRINDAVAN (*vrindāvan*): A holy place on the banks of the Yamuna River, famous as the site of Lord Krishna's youthful sport with the *gopīs*.

WHITE FLAME: *See* four lights.

WORD, THE: *See* mantra.

YAJNA (*yajña*): A sacrificial fire ritual in which Vedic mantras are recited as different woods, fruits, grains, oils, yogurt, and ghee are poured into the fire as an offering to the Lord. Also, any work or spiritual practice that is offered as worship to God.

YAJNAPRASAD (*yajñaprasāda*): (*lit.* gift of the fire ritual) The sacred ash produced by the fire ritual that is full of its sacred vibrations is often distributed to the devotees as *prasāda*; a gift of food that has been blessed as part of the offerings during the fire ritual. *See also* yajna.

YAMUNA (*yamunā*): A sacred river in north India where Lord Krishna played in His youth; site of the *raslīla*, or dance with His devotees, the milkmaids of Vrindavan.

YOGA (*yoga*): (*lit.* union) Union with God or the inner Self; a method or practice leading to that state. *See also* bhakti yoga, hatha yoga, jnana yoga, karma yoga, laya yoga, mantra yoga, raja yoga, Siddha Mahayoga.

YOGA VASISHTHA (*yoga vāsishtha*): A very popular 12th century B.C. work of non-dual philosophy ascribed to the sage Valmiki, in which the sage Vasishtha answers Lord Rama's questions about life, death, and human suffering. It teaches that the world is as you see it, and that illusion ceases when the mind is stilled.

Glossary

YOGA-TANTRAS (*yoga-tantras*): An esoteric spiritual discipline, described in works called *tantras*, in which Shakti, the creative power of the Absolute, is worshiped as the divine Mother for the attainment of Self-realization.

YOGASHAKTI (*yogashakti*): The power of yoga that is the Goddess Kundalini Shakti.

YOGINI (*yogini*): A female practitioner of yoga; in verse 105, the great Goddess Herself. *See also* Chiti; Kundalini; Shakti; Yogashakti.

YOGI(S) (*yogī*): A male practitioner of *yoga,* who through the practices of *yoga* attains higher states of consciousness.

Further Reading

SWAMI MUKTANANDA

Play of Consciousness
From the Finite to the Infinite
Where Are You Going?
I Have Become Alive
The Perfect Relationship
Reflections of the Self
Secret of the Siddhas
I Am That
Kundalini
Mystery of the Mind
Does Death Really Exist?
Light on the Path
In the Company of a Siddha
Lalleshwari
Meditate

SWAMI CHIDVILASANANDA

My Lord Loves a Pure Heart
Kindle My Heart
Ashes at My Guru's Feet

You may learn more about the teachings and
practices of Siddha Yoga Meditation by contacting:

SYDA Foundation
371 Brickman Rd.
PO Box 600
South Fallsburg, NY
12779-0600, USA
Tel: (914) 434-2000

or

Gurudev Siddha Peeth
P.O. Ganeshpuri
PIN 401 206
District Thana
Maharashtra, India

For further information about books in print
by Swami Muktananda and Swami Chidvilasananda,
and editions in translation, please contact:

Siddha Yoga Meditation Bookstore
371 Brickman Rd.
PO Box 600
South Fallsburg, NY
12779-0600, USA
Tel: (914) 434-0124